Shay Pendray's Needlecraft Projects

from The Embroidery Studio

Shay Pendray's Needlecraft Projects

from The Embroidery Studio

Sterling Publishing Co., Inc. New York
A Sterling/Chapelle Book

For Chapelle Limited

Owner:

Jo Packham

Editor:

Leslie Ridenour

Staff:

Joy Anckner, Malissa Boatwright, Sara Casperson,
Rebecca Christensen, Amber Hansen, Holly Hollingsworth,
Susan Jorgensen, Susan Laws, Amanda McPeck,
Barbara Milburn, Pat Pearson, Cindy Rooks, Cindy Stoeckl,
Ryanne Webster and Nancy Whitley

Photographer:

Kevin Dilley for Hazen Photography

Photo Stylists: Cherie Herrick and Susan Laws

Library of Congress Cataloging-in-Publication Data

Pendray, Shay.
    [Needlecraft projects]
    Shay Pendray's needlecraft projects / by Embroidery Studio.
        p.   cm.
    "A Sterling/Chapelle book."
    Includes index.
    ISBN 0-8069-4864-7
    1. Embroidery. 2. Embroidery—Patterns. I. Embroidery
studio (Television program) II. Title.
TT770.P43   1996
746.44'041—dc20   96-15464
                                                        CIP

10 9 8 7 6 5 4 3 2 1

A Sterling/Chapelle Book

Published by Sterling Publishing Company, Inc.
387 Park Avenue South, New York, N.Y. 10016
© 1996 by Chapelle Ltd.
Distributed in Canada by Sterling Publishing
℅ Canadian Manda Group, One Atlantic Avenue, Suite 105
Toronto, Ontario, Canada M6K 3E7
Distributed in Great Britain and Europe by Cassell PLC
Wellington House, 125 Strand, London WC2R 0BB, England
Distributed in Australia by Capricorn Link (Australia) Pty Ltd.
P.O. Box 6651, Baulkham Hills, Business Centre, NSW 2153,
Australia
Printed in Hong Kong & bound in China
All Rights Reserved

Sterling ISBN 0-8069-4864-7

Special thanks are extended to the following artists
who allowed us to use their fine original jewelry and
boxes as props for the photographs in this book:

Joan Carson, page 8

John Russell, page 15

Ervin Somogyi, page 31

Joel Gelfand, page 38

Lori Glick, pages 1 and 51

William McDowell, page 72

Harriet Forman Barrett (jewelry), pages 72 and 123

Bill and Nan Bolstad, page 80

Merry Lee Rae (jewelry), page 80

Ken Shepard, pages 85 and 114

Judy Ditmer, page 89

Peter Bull, page 92

Terry Evans, page 105

Doug Muscannell and Karen Harbaugh, page 109

Mark Rehmar, page 112

Eugene Watson, page 123

Eric Arcese, page 125

Alison Stern (jewelry), page 125

If you have any questions or comments or would like
information about any specialty products featured in this
book, please contact:

Chapelle Ltd., Inc.
PO Box 9252
Ogden, UT 84409

Phone: (801) 621-2777
FAX: (801) 621-2788

THE EMBROIDERY STUDIO

*P*AT ROZENDAL *(left)* is "The Embroidery Studio's" originator of the "Footnotes" segments of the series. As a certified master needlework judge through The Embroiderers' Guild of America, she is a national teacher and lecturer. A master craftsperson in canvas work, she has a diverse background in design, history and techniques, with a special interest in antique samplers.

*S*HAY PENDRAY *(right)* is certified as a teacher in Canvas Work by The Embroiderer's Guild of America and has also taught classes for The American Needlepoint Guild, The Council of Canadian Embroiderer's Guild, The American Professional Needlework Retailers and other professional corporations.

In addition to embroidery, she also teaches business classes and a professional teacher's class. Shay brings her vast knowledge to television as host of the Public Broadcast Series, "The Embroidery Studio." She has given hundreds of seminars around the world and has also authored the book *Stitching Toward Perfection*.

*T*HE EMBROIDERY STUDIO", is a 13-part "how-to" television series for stitching enthusiasts. As a companion to this program this book presents the theme of "Color in Embroidery."

Host Shay Pendray, respected teacher, author and lecturer, and Pat Rozendal, producer/technical coordinator, travel throughout the country visiting museums of historical interest to embroiderers and bringing viewers the latest techniques used by renowned needle artists.

Some of the techniques demonstrated in the series include ribbon embroidery, canvas work, Japanese embroidery, surface stitching, counted cross-stitch and more.

The program also features a painted canvas to embellish, a visit to a museum in Florida to watch Koyo Kida conduct a traditional Japanese embroidery class, a demonstration of overdying and a visit to the Chicago studios of fiber artist, Barbara Smith.

"The Embroidery Studio" is a production of WKPC-TV, Louisville, Kentucky.

THE EMBROIDERY STUDIO

$\mathscr{C}$ontents

COLOR IN EMBROIDERY

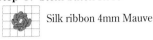

HARDANGER WREATH

ℰ MIE BISHOP spent the first part of her adult life teaching high school history and English in Utah and Maryland. After her husband, Mike, finished his education, they returned to Cache Valley, Utah so that he could begin his career. During the busy years of raising the family (Marion, Eric, Matt, Mark and Scott), she found time to attend art classes.

Designing, she says, is a natural combination of her experience in all types of needlework as well as her love of art. Emie began designing professionally 14 years ago. Since that time, she has published more than 105 books and leaflets. Her designs have also appeared in a variety of magazines and other publications. Two of her publications, No. 83 Noel and No. 96 Embellishments, have won the coveted Ginnie award.

Emie's design style employs a variety of needlework techniques. She uses cross-stitch for images and color. To add texture and depth, she uses Hardanger, pulled work, ribbon embroidery, and several other historic stitches.

In addition to trade shows, she attends one consumer show each year so that she can teach and share her enthusiasm for needlework. She takes great pleasure in helping others expand their knowledge.

Some of Emie's other pursuits include running, camping, skiing, quilting, and spending time with her family.

Stitched on cream Belfast linen 32 over 2 threads, the finished design size is 3⅜" x 9". The fabric was cut 10" x 15".

Stitches are worked in horizontal sections from the top of the sampler to the bottom. See pages 20 to 22 for stitches.

Fabric	Design Size
Aida 11	4⅞" x 13"
Aida 14	3⅞" x 10¼"
Aida 18	3" x 8"
Hardanger 22	2½" x 6½"

Section 1
Anchor   DMC

Step 1: Cross-Stitch (2 strands)

		DMC	
1016		778	Antique Mauve–vy. lt.
1017		3727	Antique Mauve–lt.
969		316	Antique Mauve–med.
1019		3726	Antique Mauve–dk.
859		3052	Green Gray–med.
846		3051	Green Gray–dk.

Step 2: Backstitch (2 strands)

859		3052	Green Gray–med.

Step 3: Bullion Stitch (1 strand)

1016		778	Antique Mauve–vy. lt.

Step 4: Hardanger (1 strand)

387		Pearl cotton #8 Ecru (kloster blocks)
387		Pearl cotton #12 Ecru (woven bars)
387		Pearl cotton #12 Ecru (woven bars with dove's eye)
387		Pearl cotton #12 Ecru (woven bars with buttonhole bar)

Step 5: Beading Stitch

		Seed 11/0 Pale Blue

Step 6: Stem Stitch Rose

 Silk ribbon 4mm Mauve

Section 2
Overdyed Pearl Cotton #12

Step 1: Satin Stitch (1 strand)

	Lilac shades

Section 3
Anchor   DMC Pearl Cotton #8

Step 1: Satin Stitch (1 strand)

387		Ecru

Section 4
Anchor   DMC

Step 1: Cross-Stitch (2 strands)

1016		778	Antique Mauve–vy. lt.
969		316	Antique Mauve–med.
859		3052	Green Gray–med.

Step 2: Stem Stitch Rose

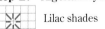 Silk ribbon 4mm Mauve

Section 5
Overdyed Pearl Cotton #12

Step 1: Reverse Scotch Stitch (1 strand)

	Lilac shades

Step 2: Algerian Eye Stitch (1 strand)

	Lilac shades

Section 6
Anchor   DMC Pearl Cotton #12

Step 1: Diamond Filling Stitch (1 strand)

387		Ecru

Section 7

Anchor   DMC

Step 1: Cross-Stitch (2 strands)

969   316   Antique Mauve–med.

859   3052 Green Gray–med.

Step 2: Backstitch (2 strands)

859   3052 Green Gray–med.

Step 3: Hardanger (1 strand)

387   Pearl cotton #8 Ecru
             (kloster blocks)

387   Pearl cotton #12 Ecru
             (woven bars)

387   Pearl cotton #12 Ecru
             (woven bars with picots)

387   Pearl cotton #12 Ecru
             (woven bars with
             spider web)

HARDANGER WREATH   TOP   **Stitch Count: 54 x 143**   **Each grid square = 2 threads**

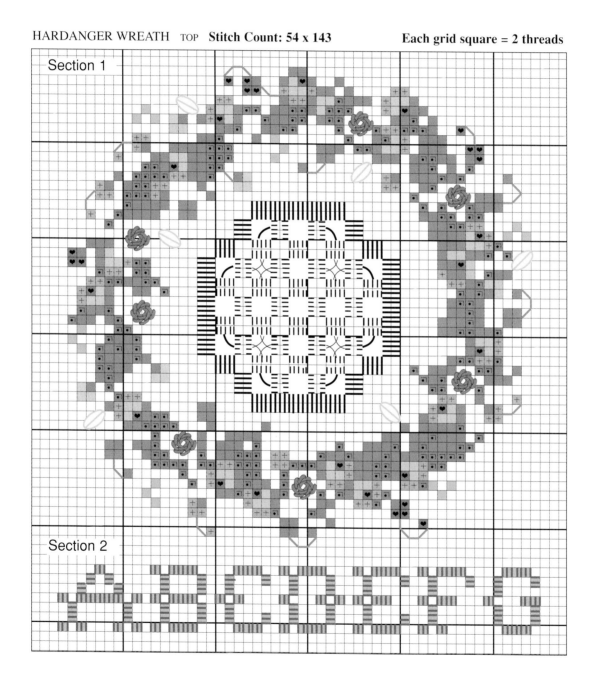

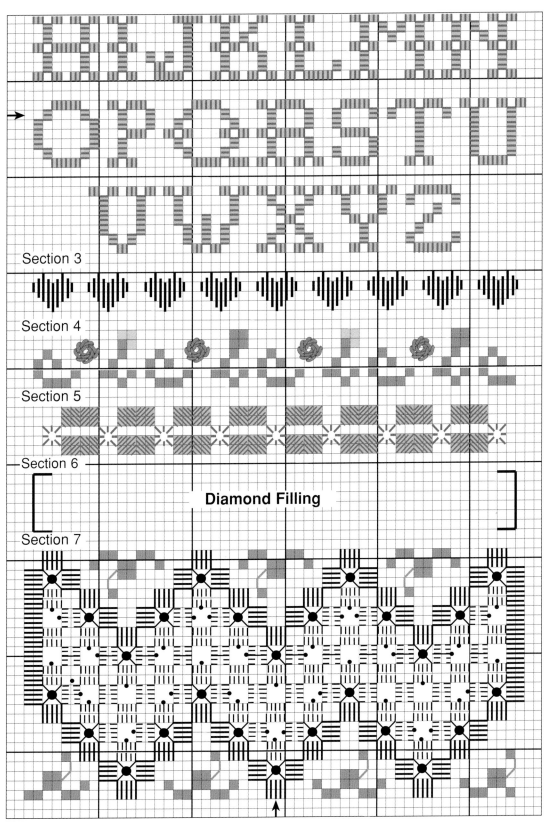

Section 3

Section 4

Section 5

Section 6

Diamond Filling

Section 7

HARDANGER WREATH   BOTTOM

ROCKOME

Stitched on Natural linen 28 over 2 threads, the finished design size is 5⅛" x 7⅝". The fabric was cut 12" x 14" for the large sampler and 1⅜" x 1⅜" for the small sampler.

Stitches are worked in horizontal sections from the top of the sampler to the bottom. The border is worked last. See pages 20 to 22 for stitches.

For Section 9, replace the "E" and "B" at the beginning and ending of the last row with your own first and last name initials. Use Small Algerian Eye Stitch for your first name initial within the alphabet.

Large Sampler

Fabric	Design Size
Aida 11	6½" x 9¾"
Aida 18	4" x 6"
Hardanger 22	3¼" x 4⅞"

Small Sampler

Fabric	Design Size
Aida 11	1⅞" x 1⅞"
Aida 18	1⅛" x 1⅛"
Hardanger 22	⅞" x ⅞"

EILEEN BENNETT first became interested in samplers in the early 1970s. Already an antique buff, she found that the pursuit of samplers, their various stitches, and their historical significance were beginning to consume her life. She started a quest that has taken her around the country, as well as to England and Ireland, exploring museums that hold textile treasures.

Eileen feels that a more accurate picture of the past is gained through the study of antique needlework. She has dedicated her life to not only studying samplers but teaching about them as well. She has written for several national needlework publications about the subject and travels throughout the United States teaching varied workshops and seminars.

Once an owner of a cross-stitch shop, Eileen began designing when she needed a sampler that incorporated all the basic stitches that she wanted to teach. She designed the very popular "Home Is Where You Hang Your Needlework" piece. That was in 1984. Since then, she has given up her shop and turned her attention to teaching and designing, with more than 40 samplers to her credit. She has also written a book that explains more than 50 historic stitches that her many designs have reintroduced.

Section 1

Anchor   **DMC**

Step 1: Cross-Stitch (2 strands)

393   3790 Beige Gray–ultra vy. dk.

Step 2: Scotch Stitch (2 strands)

393   3790 Beige Gray–ultra vy. dk.

Step 3: Double Leviathan Stitch (2 strands)

393   3790 Beige Gray–ultra vy. dk.

Step 4: Beading Stitch

Seed 11/0 Smokey Heather

Section 2

DMC Pearl Cotton #12

Step 1: Pulled-Thread Stitch (pulled tightly)

N/A   640 Beige Gray–vy. dk.

Section 3

Flower Thread

Step 1: Cross-Stitch (1 strand)

2640 Beige Gray–vy. dk.

Section 4

Anchor   **DMC**

Step 1: Cross-Stitch (2 strands)

393   3790 Beige Gray–ultra vy. dk.

Step 2: Smyrna Cross-Stitch (2 strands)

393   3790 Beige Gray–ultra vy. dk.

Step 3: French Knot

903   640 Beige Gray–vy. dk.
Pearl cotton #12

Step 4: Satin Stitch (3 strands)

903   640 Beige Gray–vy. dk.

Section 5

Flower Thread

Step 1: Knitting Stitch

2640 Beige Gray–vy. dk.

Section 6

Anchor   **DMC**

Step 1: Cross-Stitch (2 strands)

903   640 Beige Gray–vy. dk.

Section 7

Flower Thread

Step 1: Knitting Stitch

2640 Beige Gray–vy. dk.

Section 8

DMC Pearl Cotton #12

Step 1: Four-Sided Stitch (pulled tightly)

N/A   640 Beige Gray–vy. dk.

ROCKOME LARGE SAMPLER TOP **Stitch Count: 71 x 107**   **Each grid square = 1 thread**

Section

1

2

3

4

13

Section

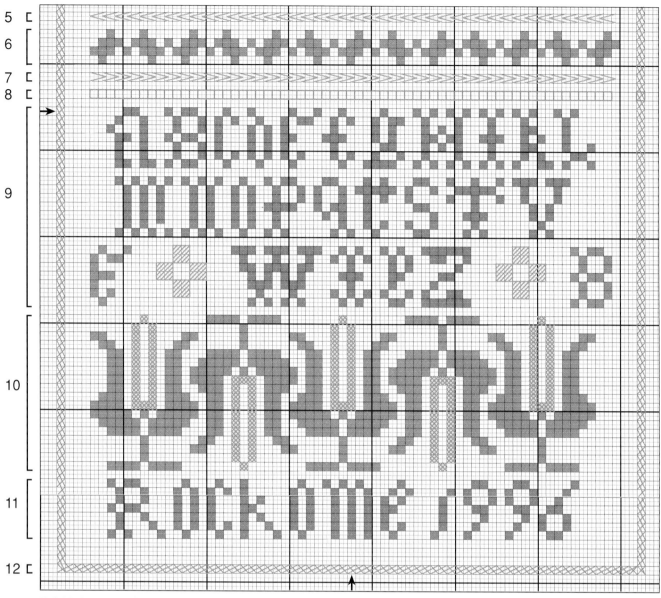

ROCKOME LARGE SAMPLER BOTTOM

Section 9

Anchor   DMC
    Step 1: Cross-Stitch (2 strands)

393   3790 Beige Gray–ultra vy. dk.
        Small Algerian Eye Stitch can be used to stitch the first initial in name.

Section 10

Anchor   DMC
    Step 1: Cross-Stitch (2 strands)

903   640 Beige Gray–vy. dk.

    Step 2: Rice Stitch (1 strand)

903   640 Beige Gray–vy. dk.

Section 11

Anchor   DMC
    Step 1: Cross-Stitch (2 strands)

393   3790 Beige Gray–ultra vy. dk.

Section 12
    DMC Pearl Cotton #12
    Step 1: Directional Long Arm Cross-Stitch

N/A   640 Beige Gray–vy. dk.

ROCKOME SMALL SAMPLER
Stitch Count: 20 x 20
Each grid square = 1 thread

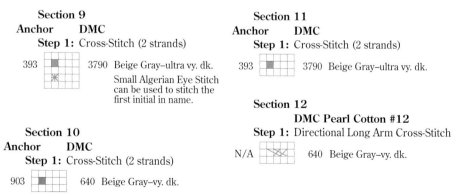

𝒯 T IS NO SURPRISE that Mary Riggs loves all kinds of needlework, having grown up in Michigan with a talented mother *(pictured left with Mary)* and two sisters. As an adult, she has been especially interested in samplers, and never tires of viewing a new collection, or placing the first stitches on a new piece of linen.

She began designing and reproducing antique samplers six years ago, while living with her family in Europe for ten years during her husband's military career. This was the start of *The Handwork Collection*, a catalog that now makes over 40 kits available.

The first pieces were German and Danish reproductions, and then original designs. Mary's most recent works include beautiful English and American reproductions. She has been allowed to work with the collections of two museums in England—The Royal Tunbridge Well Museum and The Hove Museum—as well as some extraordinary private collections.

Along with the reproductions, she has recently developed a design for a teaching sampler of stitches. It was shown at the Loudoun Museum's recent exhibit, "Threads of History," a display of local Virginia samplers, which was held in conjunction with a a lecture by Betty Ring, a noted sampler historian.

Since moving home to the Washington, D.C., area, Mary has spoken at some of the local sampler guild meetings and participated in sampler weekends on the East Coast. Her plans for the future include designing more American reproductions and possibly working with American museum collections.

BE NOT WEARY

Stitched on antique tan Belfast linen 32 over 2 threads, the finished design size is 8¾" x 9½". The fabric was cut 15" x 16".

Stitches are worked in horizontal sections from the top of the sampler to the bottom. See pages 20 to 22 for stitches.

Fabric	Design Size
Aida 11	12⅞" x 13¾"
Aida 14	10⅛" x 10¾"
Aida 18	7⅞" x 8⅜"
Hardanger 22	6⅜" x 6⅞"

Section 1

Anchor		DMC	
Step 1:	Cross-Stitch (2 strands)		
868		758	Terra Cotta–lt.
896		3721	Shell Pink–dk.
842		3013	Khaki Green–lt.
387		822	Beige Gray–lt.

Anchor		DMC	
Step 2:	Rice Stitch (2 strands)		
879		500	Blue Green–vy. dk.

Section 2

Anchor		DMC	
Step 1:	Cross-Stitch (2 strands)		
308		782	Topaz–med.
868		758	Terra Cotta–lt.

Anchor		DMC	
168		3810	Turquoise–dk.
851		924	Slate Green–vy. dk.
842		3013	Khaki Green–lt.
387		822	Beige Gray–lt.
956		613	Drab Brown–lt.
888		3828	Hazel Nut Brown
352		300	Mahogany–vy. dk.

Section 3

Anchor		DMC	
Step 1:	Satin Stitch (2 strands)		
387		822	Beige Gray–lt.

Anchor		DMC	
Step 2:	Eyelet Stitch (2 strands)		
387		822	Beige Gray–lt.

BE NOT WEARY TOP LEFT **Stitch Count: 141 x 151**   **Each grid square = 2 threads**

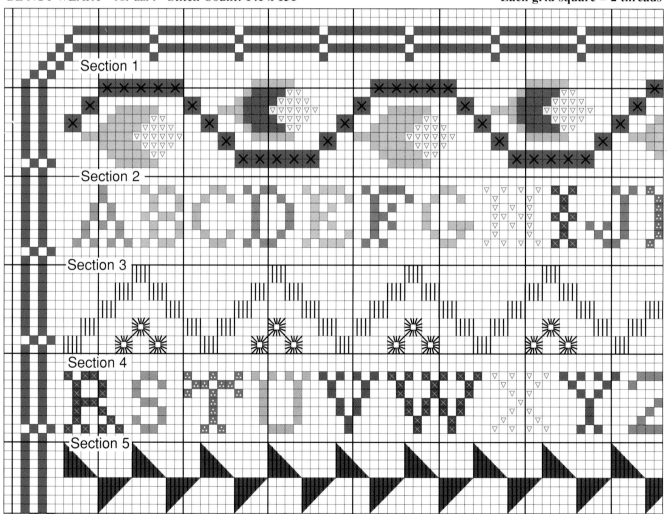

Section 4
Anchor DMC
Step 1: Cross-Stitch (2 strands)

Anchor		DMC	
308		782	Topaz–med.
896		3721	Shell Pink–dk.
851		924	Slate Green–vy. dk.
387		822	Beige Gray–lt.
956		613	Drab Brown–lt.
888		3828	Hazel Nut Brown
352		300	Mahogany–vy. dk.

Step 2: Four-Sided Stitch (2 strands)

888		3828	Hazel Nut Brown

Section 5
Anchor DMC
Step 1: Satin Stitch (2 strands)

352		300	Mahogany–vy. dk.

Section 6
Anchor DMC
Step 1: Cross-Stitch (2 strands)

Anchor		DMC	
896		3721	Shell Pink–dk.
851		924	Slate Green–vy.dk.
956		613	Drab Brown–lt.

Step 2: Diamond Eyelet (2 strands)

956		613	Drab Brown–lt.

Section 7
Anchor DMC
Step 1: Cross-Stitch (2 strands)

Anchor		DMC	
868		758	Terra Cotta–lt.
896		3721	Shell Pink–dk.
168		3810	Turquoise–dk.
842		3013	Khaki Green–lt.
879		500	Blue Green–vy. dk.
888		3828	Hazel Nut Brown

Step 2: Satin Stitch (2 strands)

387		822	Beige Gray–lt.

Step 3: Herringbone Stitch (2 strands)

387		822	Beige Gray–lt.

Step 4: Backstitch (2 strands)

308		782	Topaz–med.

Section 8
Anchor DMC
Step 1: Cross-Stitch (2 strands)

879		500	Blue Green–vy. dk.

BE NOT WEARY   TOP RIGHT

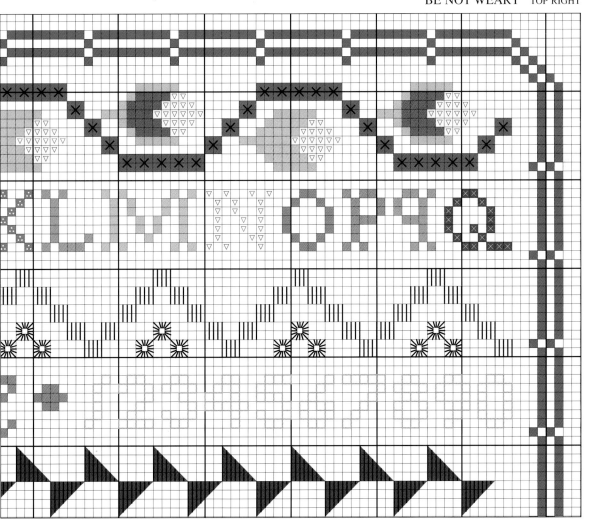

17

Section 6

Be not weary

in well doing

Section 7

Section 8

BE NOT WEARY   BOTTOM LEFT

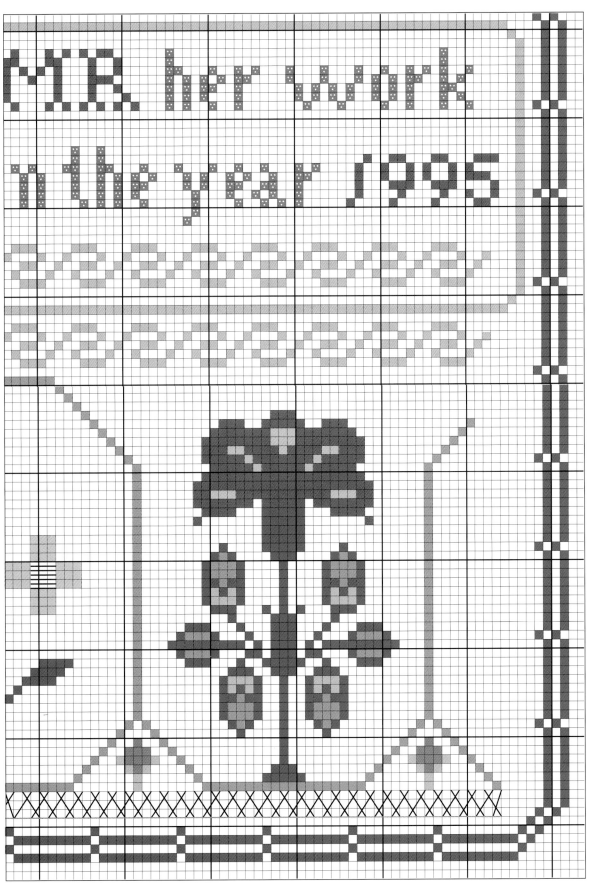

BE NOT WEARY   BOTTOM RIGHT

ALGERIAN EYE

Bring needle up at 1, down at 2, up at 3, down at 4, and up at 5. Continue around until 7 stitches have been made, all coming down into the center.

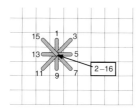

BACKSTITCH

Come up at 1 and go down at 2, to the right of 1. Come up at 3, to the left of 1. Repeat 2-3, inserting the needle in the same hole.

BEADING STITCH

Using one strand of floss, come up through fabric. Slide the bead on the needle and push the needle back down through fabric. Knot off each bead.

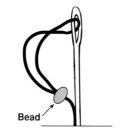

Bead

BULLION STITCH

Bring needle up at 1 and down and 2. Needle must come back up at 3 which is where it originated (1). Do not pull needle through. Wind thread around needle six or seven times. Hold the coil and needle firmly with thumb and forefinger and pull needle and thread through. Turn coil back and insert needle back into fabric at 4. To make bullion curve more, wind more thread.

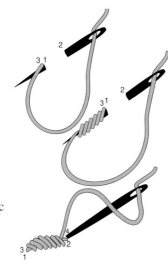

CROSS-STITCH

Come up at 1. Go down at 2. Come up at 3 and go down at 4, forming an "X". Make half-cross by coming up at 3 at mid-point of 1-2 stitch. Stitch rows as shown.

DIAMOND EYELET STITCH

This stitch consists of four sides. Bring needle up at 1 and down at 2 (center). Continue around center 12 times, bringing needle down through center each time.

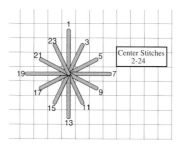

Center Stitches 2-24

DIAMOND FILLING STITCH

Work this stitch in two passes, working first (lower) row from right to left. Bring the needle up at 1 and down at 2, up at 3 and down at 4. Continue in this manner to end of row. Turn fabric around and work second row in same manner as before with connecting stitches of second row worked into same hole as stitches of first row.

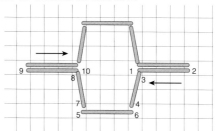

DIRECTIONAL LONG ARM CROSS-STITCH

Working from left to right, bring needle up at 1, down at 2, up at 3, down at 4, and up at 5. Continue in this manner, keeping the proportions between the long stitch and short cross the same.

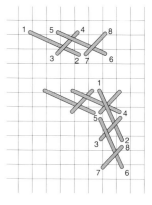

DOUBLE LEVIATHAN STITCH

Work a Cross-Stitch over four threads. Continue making intersecting stitches following diagram sequence.

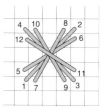

EYELET STITCH

This stitch consists of 4 sides. Bring needle up at 1 and down at 2 (center). Continue around center 16 times, bringing needle down through center each time.

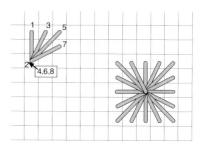

FOUR-SIDED STITCH

Come up at 1 and go down at 2. Pull threads tightly. Come up diagonally at 3 and down at 4. Come up diagonally at 5 and down at 6. Come up diagonally at 7 and down at 8.

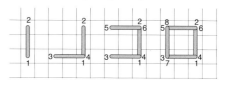

FRENCH KNOT

Come up at 1; loosely wrap once around needle. Place needle at 2, next to 1. Pull taut as you push needle down through fabric. Carry across back of work between knots.

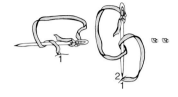

HERRINGBONE STITCH

Come up at 1, go down at 2. Go back horizontally, come up at 3, down at 4, making an "X". Come up at 5, down at 6. Come up at 7, down at 8. Continue until stitch is complete.

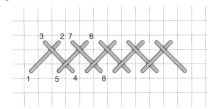

KLOSTER BLOCKS

Kloster Blocks are formed by stitching five satin stitches over four threads. Work blocks across canvas according to pattern. Complete all Kloster Blocks in a motif before cutting threads (see "Cutting Threads" below).

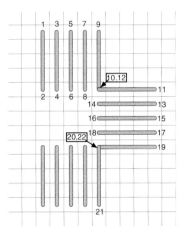

CUTTING THREADS

Before cutting any threads, be sure that there are two Kloster Blocks opposite one another. Then insert scissors under the four fabric threads next to the Satin Stitches in that block.

Cut the four threads close to the Satin Stitches; then cut the fabric threads next to the Satin Stitches of the block opposite. Cut only one area at a time. Cut ends that are visible at the edges of the block will shrink behind when the piece is washed.

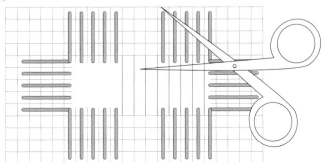

KNITTING STITCH

1. Stitching from left to right, bring needle up at 1, down at 2, crossing one higher horizontal thread. Come up at 3, and continue to desired length. To return, come up two horizontal threads below last insertion point and go down as indicated on diagram.

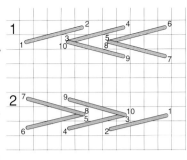

2. Work from right to left by bringing needle up at 1 and down at 2, crossing one lower horizontal thread. Complete stitch as indicated on diagram.

PULLED-THREAD STITCH

Work Satin Stitches over the desired number of threads, pulling each stitch very tightly. Patterns may be created by working shorter rows between the longer rows as shown in diagram. Work legs 1 through 12 and A through L. Work leg 1 to 2 at right, then legs M through X and resume at leg 3 to 4 at right.

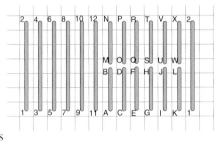

RICE STITCH

Work Cross-Stitches over four threads. Work diagonal Backstitches over the legs of each cross as shown. These may be stitched in a different color or thickness of thread.

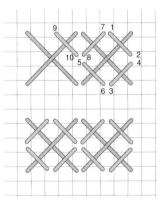

REVERSE SCOTCH STITCH & SCOTCH STITCH

This stitch consists of diagonal Straight Stitches worked over one intersection, then two, then three, then four, and back to three, two, and one. Continue in this direction for next block, or switch direction of diagonals for a Reverse Scotch Stitch.

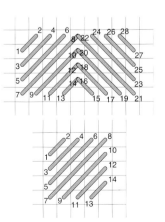

SATIN STITCH

This stitch may be worked vertically, horizontally, or on the diagonal. Stitches may be the same length or in graduations. Keeping fiber smooth and flat, come up at 1 and go down at 2, forming a Straight Stitch. Then come up at 3 and go down again at 4, forming another smooth Straight Stitch that is next to the first. Repeat to fill design area.

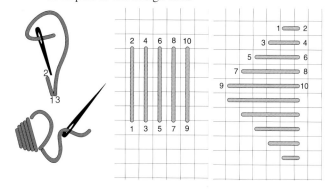

SMYRNA CROSS-STITCH

Work a Cross-Stitch. Work an upright Cross-Stitch on top. This may be done in a different color.

STEM STITCH ROSE

From left to right, make the first short stitch at the center of the rose. Come up at 1, and insert needle through fabric at 2. Bring needle up at 3 (halfway between 1 and 2), moving in a counterclockwise direction. Continue circling around the center, lengthening outer stitches until rose is completed. Take needle to back of fabric to finish.

WOVEN BAR

Use a Woven Bar to join an even number of horizontal threads after the threads above and below have been cut away (see page 21 for "Cutting Threads"). Weave needle down over top threads and up and around bottom threads as shown.

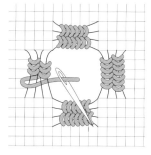

WOVEN BARS WITH BUTTONHOLE BAR

Make a foundation for buttonhole bar of two or more threads within open space. Work ordinary Buttonhole Stitches (see page 58) close together over foundation threads.

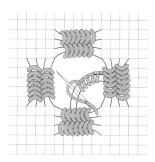

WOVEN BARS WITH DOVE'S EYE

This stitch is made up of four loops—one on each side of open space. Stitches are taken under the center stitch of the Woven Bar with the thread under the needle. Pass needle under beginning stitch and go down in fabric under center stitch of Woven Bar.

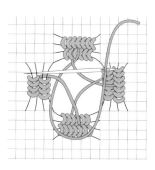

WOVEN BARS WITH PICOTS

After reaching the center of the Woven Bar, twist the thread twice around the needle clockwise and insert as shown in diagram. Hold the twisted threads with thumb still on the needle and push needle through to form a knot. Turn fabric and work second knot on other side of bar. Complete by finishing the Woven Bar.

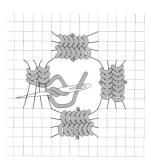

WOVEN BARS WITH SPIDER WEB

Come up at 1 and carry thread diagonally across the space, entering fabric at 2. Twist thread back over first "bar" as shown back to the starting point (3). Thread is brought back up at 4 and carried diagonally to 5 to make "spokes" across space. Twisting of this second bar is taken to the center only. The thread is then carried under and over the spokes two or three times at the center. Finish by completing twisting of thread over second bar and ending at 4.

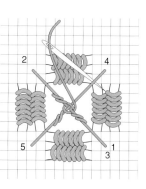

*J*EAN TAGGART is a needlework designer and teacher from Houston, Texas. Her award-winning designs have appeared in *Needle Pointers* and have been selected for the permanent collection of the Valentine Museum. Jean is a Valentine-certified canvas work teacher and serves as Director of Education for the National Academy of Needlearts. She has taught her own designs nationally for The American Needlepoint Guild, The Embroiderers' Guild of America, National Academy of Needlearts, Callaway Gardens, and The National Needlework Association Market and Needlework & Accessories Trade Show Market seminars. Jean has also authored the popular needlework book, *Laid Fillings for Evenweave Fabrics*. She is a founding partner of Brite Ideas, a corporation distributing distinctive designs and unique accessories to the needlework world.

Canvas

BEAD-DAZZLED PIN

Stitched on clear plastic canvas 14, the finished design size is 2⅛" x 2⅛". The canvas was cut 6" x 6".

Materials

Stretcher frame: 6" x 6"
Thumb tacks
Tapestry needle #22
Beading needle
Overdyed floss: blue/purple (1 skein)
Cotton & Rayon 50/50: periwinkle
    (1 skein)
Seed beads 11/0: wine (1 package)
Bugle beads #2: blue-violet
    (1 package), tropic (1 package)
Bar pin with adhesive back: 1½"
Mat board: 2" square to match
    overdyed floss
Fabric glue
Non-water-based adhesive

Notes

For other color combinations, select any overdyed floss, coordinating beads, and a solid color #5 pearl cotton. The possibilities are fantastic. Although plastic canvas is dimensionally stable, it is best to work this project with plastic mounted on a frame that can be supported by a stand to hold the frame, freeing both hands for laying stitches and handling beads.

Directions

1. Mount plastic canvas on assembled stretcher frame with thumb tacks placed approximately 3" apart.

2. Use one full strand (six plies) of overdyed floss, separated and recombined in tapestry needle, to work eight spear units, positioned as shown on the project graph (see page 37 for "Spear Stitch"). Note that two sequences are shown, each a mirror image of the other. The mauve stitch on the graph is the last one made in the unit—the top stitch.

3. Use one strand of periwinkle in tapestry needle to work the diagonal Satin Stitches surrounding spears (fine line symbols on graph). Plan stitch sequence to come up in an empty hole and go down into a filled one whenever possible.

4. Use four strands (plies) of overdyed floss, separated and recombined in tapestry needle, to work Smyrna Cross-Stitches around stitched area (see page 22 for "Smyrna Cross-Stitch"). Be sure to complete each unit before moving to the next one. Note that the top stitch of each unit is indicated by a mauve symbol on the graph.

5. Use one strand (ply) of overdyed floss in beading needle to attach blue-violet bugle beads (see page 20 for "Beading Stitch"). If the four beads forming the diagonal rows are out of alignment, pass the beading needle through all four at once in a single diagonal stitch to help straighten them.

6. Use one strand (ply) of overdyed floss in beading needle to attach wine seed beads over intersections of canvas with a Continental Stitch (see page 35 for "Continental Stitch"). Note the direction of the stitches in each section on the graph.

7. Use one strand (ply) of overdyed floss in beading needle to work a cascade of detached strands of beads on top of beaded center motif (see page 35 for "Bead Stringing").

The mauve squares on the graph indicate the placement of the strands of beads on the model. Alternating tropic and blue-violet bugles, separated by four wine seed beads, were used; strands of different lengths were

BEAD-DAZZLED PIN   Stitch Count: 29 x 29
Each grid line = 1 thread

created by using different numbers of repeats of beading pattern.

8. When beading is complete, cut stitchery from large piece of plastic canvas, leaving one "thread" intact on all four sides.

9. Use one strand of periwinkle in tapestry needle to overcast the bare "thread" surrounding embroidered design (see page 36 for "Overcast Stitch"). To achieve coverage at corners, make an extra stitch.

10. To finish into pin, apply an even coating of fabric glue to mat board and press it onto back of the stitchery. Place project face down on several layers of toweling; put a flat object larger than project (such as a book or sturdy magazine) on top of mat board; then put a 1-lb. weight (such as a can of food) on top, allowing six to eight hours to dry.

11. Attach pin back to mat board diagonally, from corner to corner, a bit above center line, with beaded strands hanging toward lower point of diamond shape. If using an adhesive-backed pin, just peel and stick. If using a regular bar pin, then use a non-water-based adhesive to adhere it to the mat board, following manufacturer's instructions.

HARLEQUIN POLE

Stitched on white Mono canvas 13, the finished design size is 9¼" x 19⅞". The canvas was cut 16" x 26".

Fabric	Design Size
Aida 11	10⅞" x 23½"
Aida 14	8⅝" x 18⅜"
Aida 18	6⅝" x 14¼"
Hardanger 22	5½" x 11¾"

Materials
Stretcher frame: 16" x 26"
Thumb tacks
#2 cord: gold (20 yds.)
Acrylic & wool 85/15 for needlepoint 13 ct.: white (10 yds.)
Cabled cotton for needlepoint 18 ct.: black (1 yd.), dk. peach (17 yds.), lavender (3 yds.), purple (3 yds.), rust (14 yds.)
Cotton & rayon 50/50: lt. gray (2 yds.), lt. green (10 yds.), med. green (10 yds.), pale peach (20 yds.), pink (5 yds.), plum (2 yds.), seafoam (6 yds.), white (10 yds.), yellow (6 yds.)
Fine 2-ply yarn for needlepoint 18 ct.: gray (1 large hank)
Heavy metallic thread for needlepoint 13 ct.: dk. green (12 yds. with yarn worked double)
Linen thread 16/2: gray (60 yds.)
Rayon ribbon for needlepoint 14–18 ct.: peach (10 yds.), white (10 yds.)

Color Key
A	Cabled Cotton for Needlepoint 18 ct., rust
B	Cabled Cotton for Needlepoint 18 ct., dk. peach
C	Rayon Ribbon for Needlepoint 14–18 ct., peach
D	Cotton & Rayon 50/50, pale peach
E	Heavy Metallic Thread for Needlepoint 13 ct., dk. green
F	Cotton & Rayon 50/50, med. green
G	Cotton & Rayon 50/50, lt. green
H	Cabled Cotton for Needlepoint 18 ct., purple
I	Cabled Cotton for Needlepoint 18 ct., lavender
J	Cotton & Rayon 50/50, yellow
K	Cotton & Rayon 50/50, plum
L	Cotton & Rayon 50/50, pink
M	Cotton & Rayon 50/50, seafoam
N	Cabled Cotton for Needlepoint 18 ct., black
O	Cotton & Rayon 50/50, lt. gray
P	#2 Cord, gold
Q	Cotton & Rayon 50/50, white A
R	Acrylic & Wool 85/15 for Needlepoint 13 ct., white B
S	Rayon Ribbon for Needlepoint 14–18 ct., white C
T	Fine 2-ply yarn for Needlepoint 18 ct., gray
U	Linen Thread 16/2, gray

ARRY KLEIN has been a part of the needlework industry for most of his life. At age 10, he started working in his mother's needlepoint store in Encino, California, after school. His love of working with his hands, along with the canvas and yarn given to him by Elsa Williams, motivated him to learn needlepoint. Enjoying the process and the gratification of the finished project, Barry began teaching classes on decorative stitches on canvas.

While completing his high school and college education, he painted a line of needlepoint called "Reflection" and joined The National Needlework Association as a wholesaler. He also designed painted lace inserts that became part of a design on knit sweaters using decorative knitting yarn for stitching yarns.

With the help of Clarice Bethel, a long-time friend and creative needlepoint designer, he established Trendsetter Needlepoint in 1989. Clarice is famous for faces and images that "spark the imagination through eyes that follow you and draw you in." The Harlequin Pole is just one in a series of designs which has been produced by Clarice for the Trendsetter Needlepoint line as well as for her own collection.

Notes

Wash hands to avoid soiling materials with skin oils. Attach canvas to stretcher bars to keep it taut. In each section, use the yarns as indicated only. The lines of the canvas are called "threads." Stitches are worked over these intersections as shown in each stitch diagram. Stitch only to the finished size of the graph.

Before stitching, dip ends of yarn into clear glue and allow to dry. This will stop yarn from untwisting or unchaining. If stitches become twisted, drop the needle and yarn from the canvas to unwind. Work as evenly as possible, using up-and-down stitching. Do not worry about keeping each stitch perfectly straight. Bury ends of threads behind stitching so they don't show.

Directions

Use corresponding section numbers provided on Harlequin Pole Graph on pages 28-30 to work design.

Section 1
Work in Continental Stitch with colors A and B (see page 35 for "Continental Stitch").

Section 2
Work in Continental Stitch with colors C and D (see page 35 for "Continental Stitch").

Section 3
Work all gold outlines, curls, bells, and details in Continental Stitch with color P (see page 35 for "Continental Stitch").

Section 4
Work eyes in Continental Stitch with colors E, N, M and Q (see page 35 for "Continental Stitch").

Section 5
Work nose, eye shadow, face accent in Continental Stitch with color O (see page 35 for "Continental Stitch").

Section 6
Work lips in Continental Stitch with colors K and L (see page 35 for "Continental Stitch").

Section 7
Work cheeks in Continental Stitch with colors L and V (see page 35 for "Continental Stitch").

Section 8
Work face in Continental Stitch with colors Q (see page 35 for "Continental Stitch").

Section 9
Work flowers in Smyrna Cross-Stitch with colors H, I and J (see page 22 for "Smyrna Cross-Stitch").

Section 10
Work leaves in Satin Stitch with colors F and G (see page 22 for "Satin Stitch").

Section 11
Work collar inset in Continental Stitch with color C (see page 35 for "Continental Stitch").

Section 12
Work middle collar in Continental Stitch with color D (see page 35 for "Continental Stitch").

Section 13
Work outer collar in Long Stitch with color R (see page 36 for "Long Stitch").

Section 14
Work underside of collar in Continental Stitch with color S (see page 35 for "Continental Stitch").

Section 15
Work collar tip edge in Continental Stitch with color A and collar tip inside in Smyrna Cross-Stitch with color P (see page 35 for "Continental Stitch" and page 22 for "Smyrna Cross-Stitch").

Section 16
Work gold section of pole in Continental Stitch with color P, rust section of pole in Diagonal Mosaic with color A, dk. green section of pole in Diagonal Mosaic with color E, and white section of pole in Diagonal Mosaic with color Q (see page 35 for "Continental Stitch" and "Diagonal Mosaic").

Section 17
Work ribbon edge in Continental Stitch with color C and stripes inside ribbon by alternating Mosaic Stitch with color D and Surface Darning with color F (see page 35 for "Continental Stitch," page 36 for "Mosaic Stitch," and page 37 for "Surface Darning").

Section 18
Work triangles horizontally in Satin Stitch with colors J and M and white between triangles vertically in Satin Stitches with color S, and use Overlock Stitch over white with color M (see page 22 for "Satin Stitch" and page 36 for "Overlock Stitch").

Section 19
Work ribbon outline in Continental Stitch with color K and inside of ribbon in Continental Stitch with colors L and O (see page 35 for "Continental Stitch").

Section 20
Work ribbon outline in Continental Stitch with color H, boxes in Mosaic with colors I and Q, and background of ribbon in Continental with color S (see page 35 for "Continental Stitch" and page 36 for "Mosaic Stitch").

Section 21
Work ribbon outline in Continental Stitch with color B, boxes in Long Star Stitch with color J, and background of ribbon in Continental Stitch with color O (see page 35 for "Continental Stitch" and page 36 for "Long Star Stitch").

Section 22
Work background of canvas in Lattice Pattern with 3-ply color T and Diamond Fill-in with color U (see page 36 for "Lattice Pattern Diagram" and page 35 for "Diamond Fill-in").

Section 23
Sew bells to canvas with color T, securing very well. Be sure to cover the stitched bell areas (see page 20 for "Beading Stitch").

HARLEQUIN POLE GRAPH TOP **Stitch Count: 120 x 258**

Each grid square = 1 thread

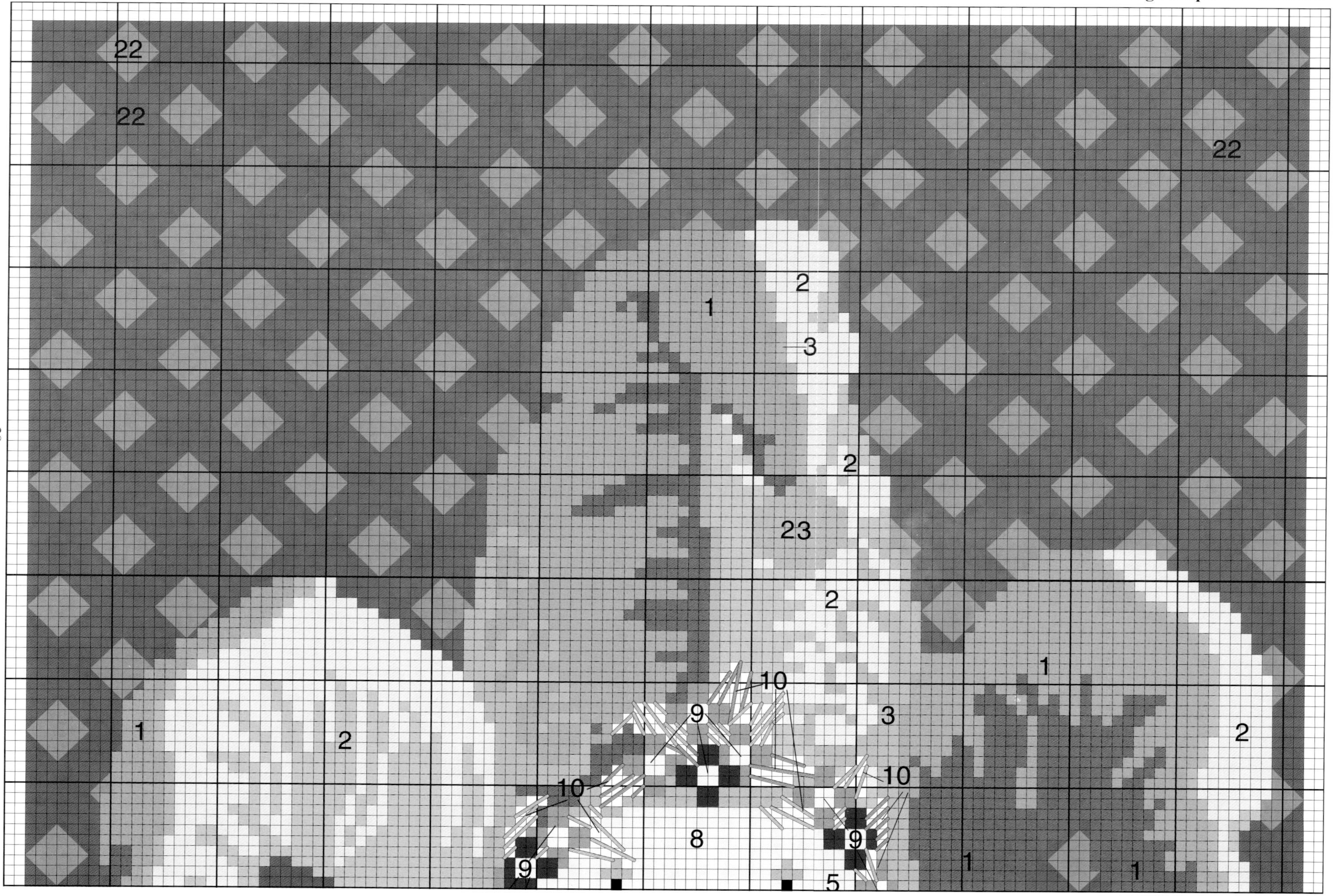

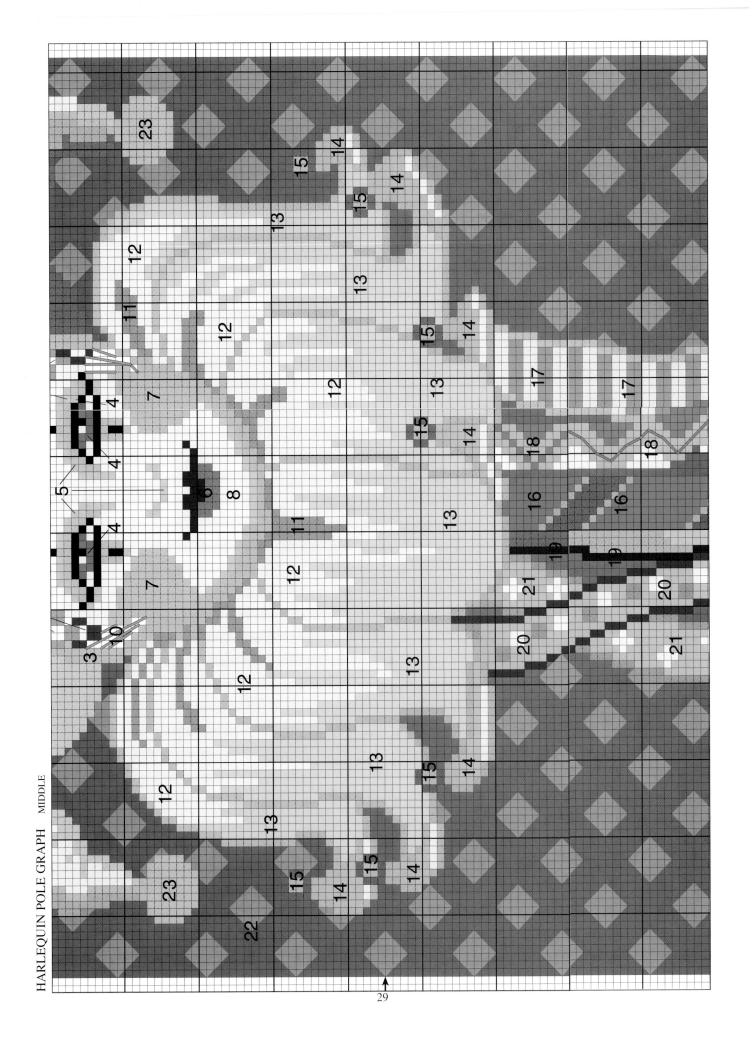

HARLEQUIN POLE GRAPH   MIDDLE

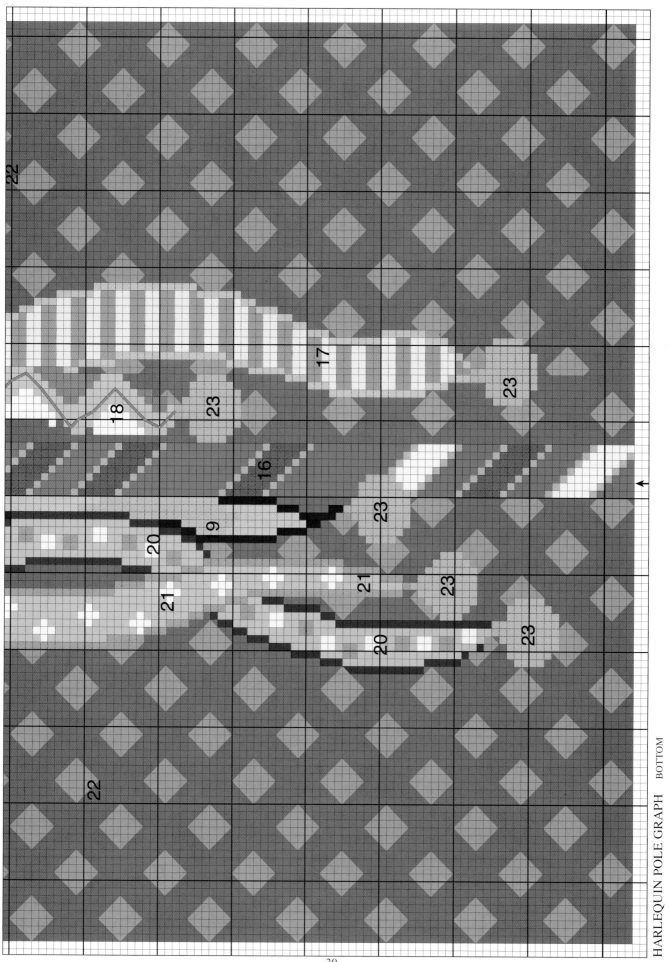

30

HARLEQUIN POLE GRAPH   BOTTOM

A NATIVE CALIFORNIAN, Jinice Beacon has spent her life in a world of sun and color. Her embroidery education started under the direction of her mother and grandmother before the age of six.

By the time she graduated from high school, she was making most of her own clothes, could knit and crochet, and had embroidered linens and completed two quilts.

At UCLA, Jinice studied art and graduated with a degree in home economics. After teaching clothing design and construction at the high school level for five years, it was time to raise a family. During this period, after exploring macrame, she discovered needlepoint. In 1969, together with her mother, Vi, she began designing for herself and friends. In 1977, she started Designs by Jinice, hand-painted needlepoint, and resumed teaching, but this time the focus was needlepoint rather than clothing construction.

Along with her love for needlepoint came involvement in The Embroiderers' Guild of America (EGA) in which she became active at chapter, regional, and national levels. Jinice continues to teach locally, and for EGA, regional and national seminars. Increasing her knowledge of canvas design and improving her techniques as well as learning and creating new stitch ideas are some of Jinice's goals. She says that the self-discipline gained through the nine steps of Traditional Japanese Embroidery under the guidance of Shuji Tamura, Elsa Cose and Shay Pendray has helped her refine her design and color ideas.

Today, her needlepoint business remains small with a limited number of new designs each year. Jinice and her mother feel that it is important to perfect each design and enjoy the process with the hope that the stitcher will be able to do the same.

JAPANESE FAN ON BLACK

Materials

Mono canvas 18 ct.: black (16" x 14")
Stretcher frame: 16" x 14"
Thumb tacks
White transfer pencil
Permanent marker fine-point: black
Tapestry needle: #22
Beading needle
Overdyed pearl cotton #5:
    blue/orange/red shades (5 yds.)
DMC Medicis: blue (3 skeins)
Rayon ribbon for needlepoint 14–
    18 ct.: dk. peach (1 card), red
    (1 card)
Suedelike yarn: red (1 card)
Rayon thread for needlepoint 18 ct.:
    aqua blue (1 skein)
DMC Fil d'Or: gold (1 spool)
Med. braid #16: red (1 spool),
    lt. blue (1 spool), silver
    (1 spool)
Fine braid #8: black (1 spool)
DMC floss: black (1 skein), 806 blue
    (1 skein), 407 lt. brown (1 skein),
    321 red (1 skein), white (1 skein)
DMC pearl cotton #5: 754 peach
    (1 skein)
Bugle beads 4½ mm: black rainbow
    (1 package)
Metallic beads 10/0: gold
    (1 package)
Cardboard: 1½" x 4"
Old toothbrush

Notes

Mount canvas on frame or stretcher bars before working design. Carefully lay ribbon fibers and multiple strands flat so they don't twist on the surface.

The eye of the needle damages metallic fibers and pearl cotton. Use short lengths, 18–24"; keep eye of needle about 3–4" from tail. Longer lengths of fibers are okay when laying lengths that will be couched down. Rayon thread is best worked doubled over in needle. Dampening fiber slightly will make it more manageable.

Refer to Japanese Fan on Black Diagram on page 34 for stitch placement. Stitch patterns up to outline marks in each section. Lines will be covered with couched braid. Beads may be attached after all stitched sections are complete. Tack on the back side to secure each bead.

Do not trail ends across open areas between or within stitched sections. When traveling from one section to another, turn the canvas and catch along outline or filled-in areas.

Directions

Using a white transfer pencil, transfer enlarged Japanese Fan on Black Diagram on page 34 to canvas. Black out any residual markings with a fine-point permanent marker. Use corresponding section numbers on diagram to work design.

Section 1A

Circular Eyelet with Bugle Beads
1. Enlarge center hole slightly to accommodate fibers. Using DMC gold 4-ply (2-ply doubled over in needle) and following numbering on diagram, stitch from outside of circle into center hole (see Circular Eyelet Diagram).

2. Add black rainbow bugle beads as shown on diagram using 2-ply DMC black floss (single strand doubled over in needle) (see page 20 for "Beading Stitch"). This step can be completed after all sections are stitched.

3. Couch one row silver braid around outer edge of circle counterclockwise, beginning at arrow marked on Circular Eyelet Diagram (see page 33 for "Couching Stitch"). End where braid meets Section 3. Use DMC white floss to couch braid. Couch 1 row red braid next to silver braid, using DMC red floss.

Section 1

Diagonal Boxes with Gold Bead
1. Create lattice using Diagonal Box Stitch silver braid, one strand (see page 35 for Diagonal Box Diagram).

2. Fill in with peach pearl cotton (see page 35 for Diagonal Box Diagram).

3. Add metallic gold bead in the center of each diamond, using sewing thread (see page 20 for "Beading Stitch").

Section 2A

Using dk. peach rayon ribbon, stitch eight-sided flower, following numbering on diagram. Stitch from the outer edge into the center. Do not allow ribbon to twist on the surface (see page 36 for Eight-Sided Flower Diagram).

Section 2B

Stitch two partial flowers as before using red rayon ribbon. Add 7–8 metallic gold beads in the center of each flower, using DMC red floss.

Section 2

Stitch background with one strand DMC gold Straight Stitches, using diagram and photo as guides for placement (see page 37 for "Straight Stitch").

Section 3

Diagonals with overdyed pearl cotton (see page 36 for Diagonal Pattern Diagram for row numbers).
1. Row 1—using DMC gold 2-ply (1-ply doubled over in the needle), work Mosaic Stitches diagonally (see page 36 for "Mosaic Stitch").

2. Row 2—use DMC lt. brown 4-ply floss to work Smyrna Cross-Stitches on top and bottom of Mosaic Stitches (see page 22 for "Smyrna Cross-Stitch" and page 36 for "Mosaic Stitch").

3. Row 3—use overdyed pearl cotton 1-ply for columns. This positions the next row of Step 2 stitches.

Section 4

Mosaic with gold metallic beads (see page 37 for Mosaic with Beads Diagram).
1. Use lt. blue braid for Mosaic Stitches (*Note:* Stitches are worked in opposite direction, as in Section 3).

2. Attach gold metallic beads with DMC blue floss.

Section 5

Woven Plaid. Stitch all rows using laid stitch method—pattern after lettering sequence on Row 1 (see page 37 for Woven Plaid Diagram). Stitch all vertical rows in each fiber, then the horizontal rows.
1. Rayon thread, 4-ply.
2. Red braid, 1-ply.
3. Dk. peach rayon ribbon.
4. Red suedelike yarn.
5. Cross Step 4 intersections with DMC gold, 2-ply.

Section 6

Rayon thread with Brick Couching in gold (see page 35 for Brick Couching Diagram).
1. With rayon thread, follow numbers on diagram, using laid stitch method.

2. Couch with DMC gold, 1 ply.

Section 7

Red braid. Fill area with horizontal Satin Stitches (see page 22 for "Satin Stitch"). Areas more than 12 threads wide can be split into two parts. Stagger to form a random pattern.

Section 8

With lt. blue braid, work Parisian Stitch (see page 37 for "Parisian Stitch").

Background

Stitch borders first. Begin and end fibers in border area. Do not trail ends across open area. Be sure to have enough fiber to make an entire trip or to an area suitable for beginning and ending threads.

1. Diagonal Lattice effect (see page 35 for Background Diagram)—using black braid, 1-ply, work rows in two trips horizontally. Follow numbers on first trip, and letters on return trip, using Double Running Stitch method (see page 57 for "Double Running Stitch").

2. Use DMC blue, 2-ply, to work vertical accent lines with black rainbow bugle beads (see page 35 for Background Diagram). Double one strand of floss over in bead needle, and attach beads as each row is stitched. Tack on back side to secure beads. Follow circled letters on diagram.

Borders

See page 35 for Background Diagram.
1. Borders a—work with red braid.
2. Border b—work with Overdyed pearl cotton, 1-ply.
3. Border c—work with Medicis, 4-ply, mitering corners.

Finishing

Couch red braid along top of fan. Couch silver braid, separating all areas not already separated by couching. Couch entire outer edge of fan and ribs. Section 3 is couched with an additional red line, using red suedelike yarn.

Cords

Create twisted cord effect using DMC floss red, 6-ply Chain Stitch. Whip with DMC floss gold, 2-ply. When whipping chain, pass needle under each link only (not through canvas). Do not allow gold to twist on the surface (see page 37 for "Whipped Chain Stitch").

Tassels

1. Cut two 4" lengths of DMC red floss and set aside. Divide remaining DMC red floss in half—one piece for each tassel. For each tassel, wind long piece of floss lengthwise around the cardboard piece.

2. Using a 4" length of red floss, slip under loops and knot at top of cardboard. Slide off cardboard. Cut loops.

3. Wrap tassel neck using gold. Wrapped area covers about ⅜". Knot ends and thread into needle, burying ends inside tassel. Using an old toothbrush, comb tassel to separate plies. Trim ragged bottom edges.

4. Using DMC blue or red floss, attach three strands of beads to each tassel under wrapped area of tassel. String beads as follows: five gold metallic, one black rainbow bugle, one gold metallic, one black rainbow bugle and one gold metallic. Using last gold metallic bead as turning bead, slip needle back up inside other beads (see page 35 for "Bead Stringing"). Cinch up strand of beads until they are snug against wrapped portion of tassel. Anchor floss by tacking, and complete two more strands. Tie off floss.

5. Thread top ends into tapestry needle, and stitch tassel to end of twisted cord. Tie ends in a knot on the back and bury ends behind twisted cord. To get tassels to stay at a slight angle, secure back side of wrapped section with a stitch from the back using DMC blue floss.

CIRCULAR EYELET DIAGRAM

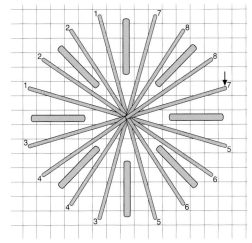

COUCHING STITCH

Complete a Straight Stitch the desired length of the design. Make sure thread is flat.

Make short tight Straight Stitches across base to "couch" the Straight Stitch (1-2). Come up on one side of the thread (3). Go down on the opposite side of the thread (4). Tack at varying intervals.

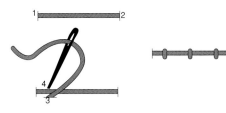

JAPANESE FAN ON BLACK DIAGRAM   Stitch Count: 210 x 182   Finished Design Size: 11¾" x 10⅛"
Enlarge 142 %

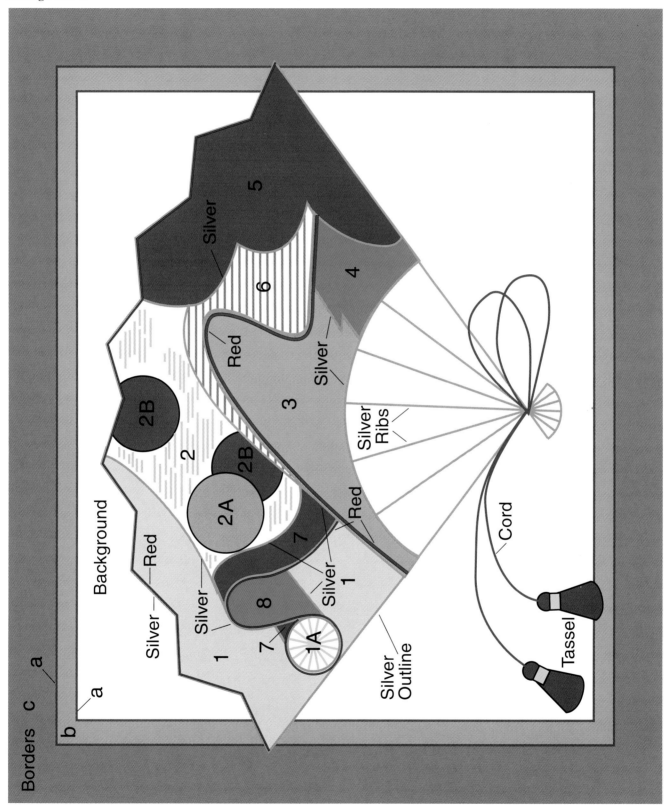

BACKGROUND DIAGRAM

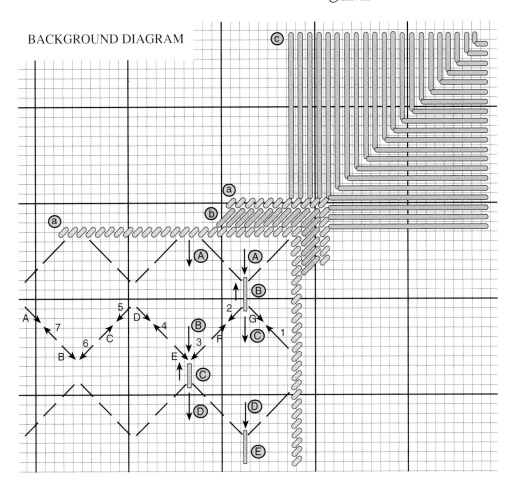

CONTINENTAL STITCH

Work in horizontal rows as shown or up and down the shape in diagonal rows, making small diagonal stitches over one intersection.

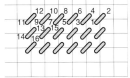

DIAGONAL MOSAIC STITCH

This stitch is worked in the same manner as the Mosaic Stitch but is stitched from bottom right up to top left on a diagonal following diagram sequence. The second row is stitched in reverse, fitting the small stitch next to the larger stitch and continuing that way.

BEAD STRINGING

Bring the needle to the front of the canvas. Thread on the desired number of beads. Without tying off the thread, reverse needle and string back through the previous bead all the way to the first. Take the needle back down through the original hole and tie off on back.

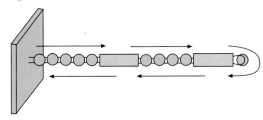

DIAGONAL BOX DIAGRAM

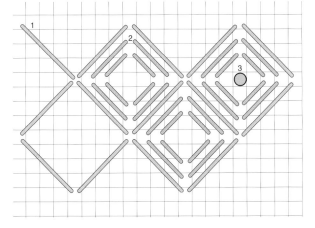

BRICK COUCHING DIAGRAM

This stitch consists of long horizontal Straight Stitches crossed at even intervals with small Straight Stitches. Stitch all long stitches first. Go back and stitch small straight stitches at even intervals along first row. For second row, work small stitches between stitches above. Repeat pattern for each row.

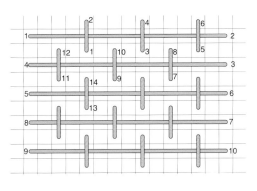

DIAMOND FILL-IN STITCH

Come up at 1 and down at 2. Bring needle back up at 3 (one thread over and one thread up from the bottom right). Insert needle at 4 (one thread over and one thread down from the top left). Continue working stitches to 12.

DIAGONAL PATTERN DIAGRAM

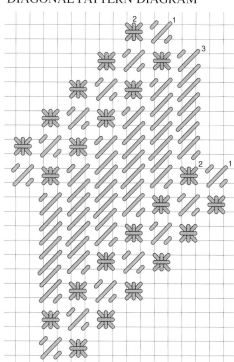

LATTICE PATTERN DIAGRAM

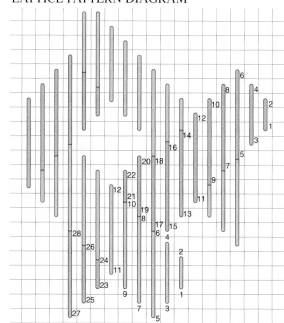

OVERCAST STITCH

This stitch is used to finish raw edges. Bring needle up at 1, wrap thread over fabric edge at 2. Bring needle back up at 3. Repeat.

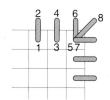

EIGHT-SIDED FLOWER DIAGRAM

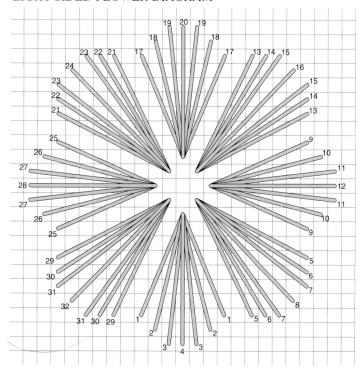

LONG STITCH

This stitch consists of Straight Stitches worked over two or more threads traveling across fabric, in an upright cross, or as shown in diagram. Follow numbering sequence to complete pattern of stitches that are the same length but alternating threads crossed every other stitch.

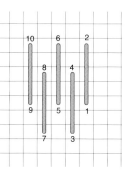

MOSAIC STITCH

This stitch is used to make a pattern of tiny square blocks. Each block consists of a diagonal stitch worked over two vertical and two horizontal threads in the center and two short diagonal stitches on each side. Work from right to left, following sequence in diagram.

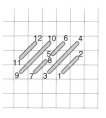

OVERLOCK STITCH

This stitch consists of a long Straight Stitch over three vertical threads and a small diagonal Straight Stitch worked just to the left of center of long stitch and across to the right over one thread. Stitch from bottom left to top right at a diagonal, working long stitches first, then making another pass

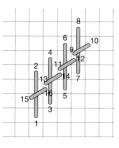

LONG STAR STITCH

This stitch consists of two parallel Straight Stitches worked vertically over three horizontal threads and crossed with two parallel Straight Stitches over three vertical threads. Follow stitch sequence as shown in diagram.

MOSAIC WITH BEADS DIAGRAM

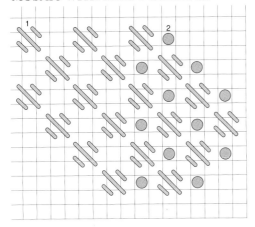

PARISIAN STITCH

This stitch consists of Straight Stitches alternately worked over four and two horizontal threads of canvas. Each row is worked alternating the length of the stitches to fit in with the preceeding row.

SPEAR STITCH

Spear stitches are long straight stitches that cross each other in the sequence shown in diagram.

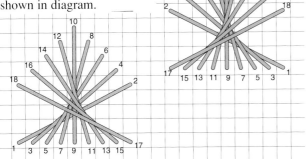

STRAIGHT STITCH

This stitch may be taut or loose, depending on desired effect. Come up and go down upon achieving desired length.

SURFACE DARNING

First work a foundation of vertical Satin Stitches over area to be covered. Weave thread between these stitches horizontally.

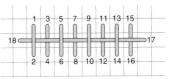

WHIPPED CHAIN STITCH

Refer to page 57 for "Chain Stitch".

To whip, use a new thread. Come up through fabric under first link in chain. Whip thread over inter-section of next link. Take thread under this link, but not through fabric, and come up on the opposite side. Continue until end of chain.

WOVEN PLAID DIAGRAM

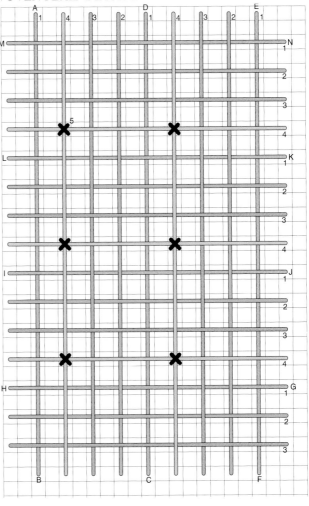

$\mathcal{F}$OR LIZ TURNER DIEHL, creativity is a movable feast. It's what has fueled her success from the plains of Kansas to the South Hills of Eugene, Oregon. It's a path ranging from spending 10 years with a symphony orchestra to owning a retail shop to orchestrating the workings of a successful, still growing international wholesale needlework business.

As owner of Designs by Liz Turner Diehl, Inc., Liz designs patterns and markets products around the world, including Hong Kong and Australia. She attends numerous trade shows across the country, enjoying the immediate reaction and feedback to her creativity that the buyers provide. Liz's creativity comes naturally. Her great-grandfather designed 15 court-houses in Kansas; her mother and grandmother were involved with needle arts and painting. Liz, herself, also has a degree in music.

In between her successful ventures and business travels, she has done a considerable amount of teaching through the Continuing Education Program in Kansas and retail stores. She has even found time left over to enjoy favorite family activities—boating and going to the beach.

assels

BLUE METALLIC

Materials
Wooden spool, hollow: 2" H x 1½"
Wooden disc: 1¼"
Spray adhesive
Cardboard: 3" x 6½"
Metallic polyester & nylon 60/40 4-ply
    with twist: gold
Rayon metallic #8: red (1 spool)
Rayon metallic #8: purple (1 spool)
Rayon metallic #8: blue (1 spool)
Rayon metallic #8: green (1 spool)
Braided cord #6: antique gold
    (2 bobbins)
Tacky glue
100% stranded silk: navy blue
    (2 packages)
Rayon metallic twist #30: antique
    gold (1 bobbin)
Nylon garland: blue (2 bobbins)

Notes
Monks Cord is twisted braid resembling the cord Monks wear around their robes. Easily handmade with any continuous yarn or fiber, Monks Cord is a perfect way to customize your work. Match the same or complementary colors, yarns, or fibers to that of your needlework. Add the finishing touch to all needlework projects with Monks Cord.

To create a larger cord in circumference, begin with more strands than three. Try blending different yarns and fibers for a special look.

Directions
1. Cover head area with light coat of spray adhesive. Wrap fiber around spool head (see Spool Head Diagram).

2. Make Monks Cord using braided cord, red rayon metallic plus purple rayon metallic, and blue rayon metallic plus green rayon metallic. Use two strands of each color.

3. For standard-size Monks Cord, calculate length of fiber needed before twisting by multiplying finished length desired by seven.

4. Fold entire length in thirds, and tie a knot at each end.

5. Insert a pencil in front of knots at each end. This requires two people (see page 40 for Monks Cord Diagram).

6. Stand facing one another. Keep fiber taut at all times. Each person begins turning his or her pencil in a clockwise direction. Turn pencils until fiber is twisted so tightly that it begins to double back on itself just near knots. Keep taut or it will kink.

7. When twisting is complete, find approximate center of fiber. One person holds the center, while the other person pulls the two pencils together, always keeping fiber taut.

8. After pencils are joined, the center person begins to let go, a few inches at a time. The fiber will naturally twist.

9. Upon reaching the pencils, remove pencils and tie knotted ends together.

10. Wrap Monks Cord vertically around spool, going through center hollow core to secure. Secure with glue on inside (see Spool Head Diagram—black stripe).

11. Using one strand of braided cord, as it comes off the spool, wrap next to Monks Cord, securing to inside of wooden spool with glue (see Spool Head Diagram—gold stripe).

12. Using 4-ply navy blue stranded silk, wrap eight even spokes around disc through center hole (see page 40 for Disc Diagrams).

13. Beginning at center with 4-ply navy blue stranded silk, stitch Ribbed Spider Web Stitch (see page 40 for Disc Diagrams) and continue until completing ¼". Change to blue rayon metallic, and stitch around twice. Change to gold metallic polyester & nylon, and stitch around twice.

Continue with 4-ply navy blue stranded silk to edge.

14. Make skirt of tassel by using all four colors of rayon metallic. Gather ends of all four colors together. Wrap over cardboard in direction of arrow so that vertical length of tassel is 6½" length (see page 40 for Skirt Diagrams).

15. Using Monks Cord directions in Steps 3–9, make cording for hanger from five strands of braided cord.

16. Use cording made in Step 15 to tie skirt of tassel together (see page 40 for Skirt Diagrams). Slip cording under one side of cardboard. Tie knot in cording, forming a loop. Pull tassel off of cardboard (see page 40 for Skirt Diagrams).

17. Move knot around so that it is buried in skirt of tassel. Pull Monks Cord up through spool. Thread through center of disc. Pull tightly. Skirt will ease up into spool slightly. Disc at top will help secure everything in place (see Spool Head Diagram and page 40 for Skirt Diagrams).

18. Separate top layer of skirt. *Hint:* Wrap a piece of paper around bulk of tassel not being used. This simply gets it out of the way, while making small tassels. Wrap with gold rayon metallic twist. Divide to be able to finish with six small tassels around skirt (see page 40 for Small Tassels Diagram).

19. Wrap blue nylon garland around neck. Fill in between skirt and decorated head area. Wrap around disc at top to fill in any bare area (see page 40 for Finished Blue Metallic Diagram).

SPOOL HEAD DIAGRAM

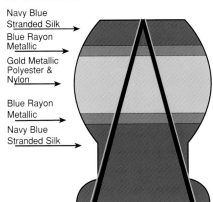

Navy Blue Stranded Silk
Blue Rayon Metallic
Gold Metallic Polyester & Nylon
Blue Rayon Metallic
Navy Blue Stranded Silk

MONKS CORD DIAGRAM

SMALL TASSELS DIAGRAM

DISC DIAGRAMS

SPOOL
HEAD &
SKIRT
DIAGRAMS

FINISHED
BLUE METALLIC
DIAGRAM

SKIRT DIAGRAMS

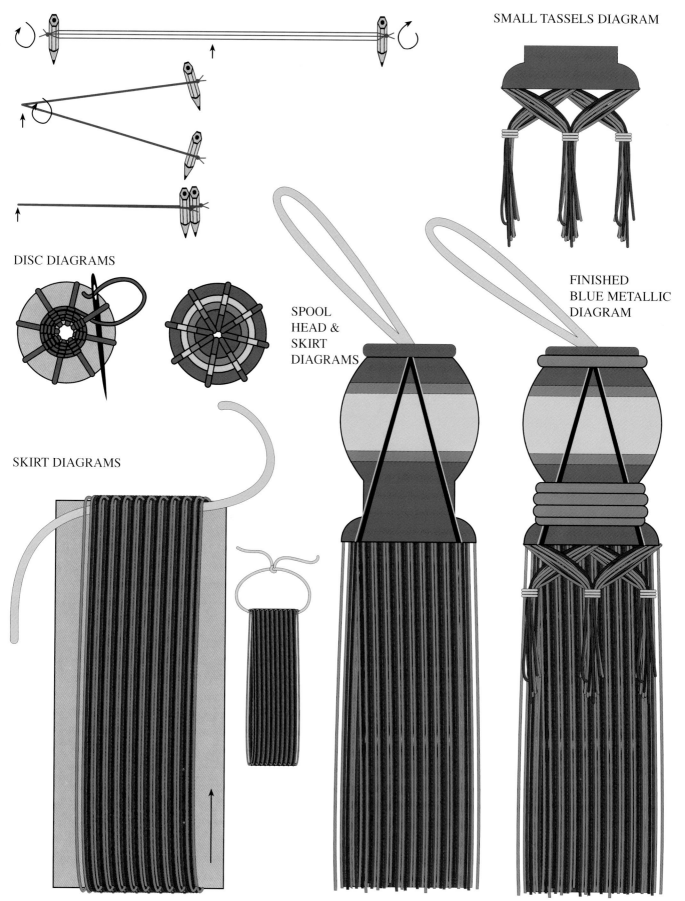

*K*IMBERLY CRUM began her career at The Art Institute of Pittsburgh, where she majored in fashion illustration and graphics. Upon graduating, she freelanced for several shops and did some design work for a couple of studios.

One day she found herself in a yarn shop overwhelmed by a desire to work with fibers. She worked at that shop for several years, gaining a great deal of knowledge. Soon she was designing sweaters for herself and customers. Several years later, she discovered a shop full of wonderful fibers and canvas work in the Boston area. She was instantly hooked and took home a tassel booklet and a handful of different fibers. When she next showed up at the shop with a newly designed tassel, the shop owner was thrilled and said, "You have to teach a class." That was almost five years ago.

Kimberly now lives in the Huntsville, Alabama, area with her husband, daughter and son. She teaches classes at a local shop and for different guilds. Aside from the tassel craze, she also designs needlepoint pieces and is currently releasing a series of petit-point pin patterns. These are multifibered, beaded affairs that she has been urged to chart and release for some time. Everyone seems to love wearable art these days, so she is hoping they will do wonderfully.

AUTUMN FIRE

Materials

Overdyed pearl cotton #5: 2 skeins
Pearl cotton #3: 3 skeins
Rayon thread for needlepoint 18 ct.:
    3 skeins
Persian yarn, 3-ply (used as 2-ply):
    1 skein
Medium braid #16: 1 spool
Fine braid #8: 1 spool
Soie d'Alger stranded silk: 1 hank
Beading thread
Seed beads 11/0: bronze (1 package)
Pebble beads: 8
Cardboard: 7" square
Large-toothed comb
Cup hook
Scissors

Making a Barber Pole Twisted Cord

1. Double over a 50" length of overdyed pearl cotton. Quadruple-fold a 100" length of medium braid. Combine resulting six strands, and knot them all together at one end. Then separate overdyed pearl cotton strands from medium braid strands. Knot end of each fiber group with an overhand knot. Hook one end to a stationary spot (cup hook or a friend). Holding the other end, begin twisting in the direction of twist of fiber.

2. If working alone, slide scissors or a heavy key ring to the center and carefully walk to the stationary spot where the twisted cord may be allowed to dangle and twist on itself. If a friend is helping, the friend should take the center knot away from the stationary spot. Knot the two ends together, and slowly release the tension a few inches at a time, allowing the cord to twist on itself.

3. Knot two loose ends together, forming a ring with the cord. Set aside.

Making the Tassel

1. Any fibers to be used in base of tassel should be rolled into separate balls, if not already in a pull skein

form. This allows drawing from each, while winding tassel around cardboard. Mark bottom of card with an arrow, and begin and end all fibers at the bottom (see Making Tassel Diagram).

2. Using all base fibers, wrap tassel around a 7" piece of sturdy cardboard until rayon thread and overdyed pearl cotton are gone and only pearl cotton #3 and Persian yarn remain.

3. Slip a long piece of pearl cotton #3 under one side, and slide up to top. Make a loose half knot to help keep track of the center. Cut across bottom with a sharp pair of scissors (see Tying Tassel Diagram).

4. Carefully lay down tassel and tighten half knot. Then turn tassel over and make another half knot. This should not move or loosen. Finish by tying off second half of knot.

5. Slip tassel through Barber Pole ring. Make sure cord knot is centered and well hidden in tassel. Make an overhand knot at top of tassel and secure it tightly (see Positioning Cord Diagrams).

6. Straighten out fibers by spritzing with water and combing out with a large-toothed comb. When all are lying nicely, tie off two necks using a half knot on one side and a double on the other. The first tie-off is about ½" down from the top. The second is about 1" down from the first.

7. Evenly trim off bottom of tassel. In preparation for embellishment, secure skirt with a bit of thread. Using a long strand of 2-ply silk, knot end and thread through beading needle. Come up through center of skirt and out just below upper neck tie-off.

Beaded Buttonhole

1. This stitch is worked between the two tie-offs. Complete first round by beginning at upper neck and working down. Catch needle in neck tie-off. Stitch about ¼" apart and end a little less than that away from first stitch (see Beaded Buttonhole Diagrams).

2. Upon returning to beginning, start taking up one seed bead before working the stitch. Push bead just off the end of needle, and gently pull down on the stitch from previous row, forming a triangle. On all following rows, a diamond will form. Catch a tiny amount of the head with each stitch and continue working Buttonhole stitch around. As each stitch is worked, bead will pop into place. Keep stitches taut but not tight (it is helpful to keep a thumb on bead as next stitch is worked).

3. As stitching nears the bottom neck tie-off, end beading and catch needle into tie-off to secure and run thread up through head to finish.

Turkey Work

Begin work where Beaded Buttonhole began, and work upward to top knot. Using 2-ply Persian yarn, complete stitches as if on canvas (see Turkey Work Diagram). Remember that wherever a stitch would be taken under a canvas thread, a small amount of tassel fibers will be caught. Make loops a good size and as uniform as possible. Larger is easier and a relaxed stitch results in a fuller effect.

Wrapping the Neck

1. Using medium #16 braid, thread needle directly from spool; do not cut. Take needle down over neck tie-off and into skirt, pulling to a point where it can be held. Remove needle, knot end, and pull back up into tassel skirt. In doing so, there is ample thread to wrap neck and no worry of running short. When wrapping, threads should lay right next to each other with no overlapping (see Finished Autumn Fire Diagram).

2. After wrapping about 1" of tassel, cut fiber and thread needle, allowing length to finish off. Run end back up behind wrap and out at top, clipping closely. Repeat this step as desired, using a different color. Thread directly from spool again, but run end up behind previous wrapping and continue to wrap in new color and finish as before.

Construct Mini-Tassels

1. Combining about 12" of several fibers, thread through four pebble beads. Slide beads apart so that they are 2" between beads and 2" from ends. Cut between beads to separate. Each bead will end up with 2" of fiber. Place bead in center of 2" length, fold fibers down, and tie a simple neck with 2-ply floss on each mini-tassel (see Mini-Tassels Diagram).

2. Knot one end of an 18" length of beading thread, lose knot in tassel, and come out at bottom of neck wrapping. String mini-tassels' beads with various seed beads at four intervals so that strand fits around tassel as a necklace. Take necklace around tassel, and run needle back through first couple of beads. Secure thread in tassel.

3. Knot one end of an 18" length of beading thread, lose knot in tassel, and come out at top of the neck wrapping. String various seed beads with four pebble beads at four intervals so that strand fits around tassel as before. Take necklace around tassel at top of neck wrapping, and run needle back through first couple of beads. Secure thread in tassel (see Finished Autumn Fire Diagram).

Wrap Neck of Each Mini-Tassel

1. Knot one end of a piece of fine #8 braid, and run down behind neck to lose knot. Bring needle out behind one of the mini-tassels. Wrap each neck four times with no overlapping. Wrap one; then sneak into tassel skirt to next mini-tassel and repeat (see Finished Autumn Fire Diagram).

2. When complete, trim skirts of mini-tassels to same length.

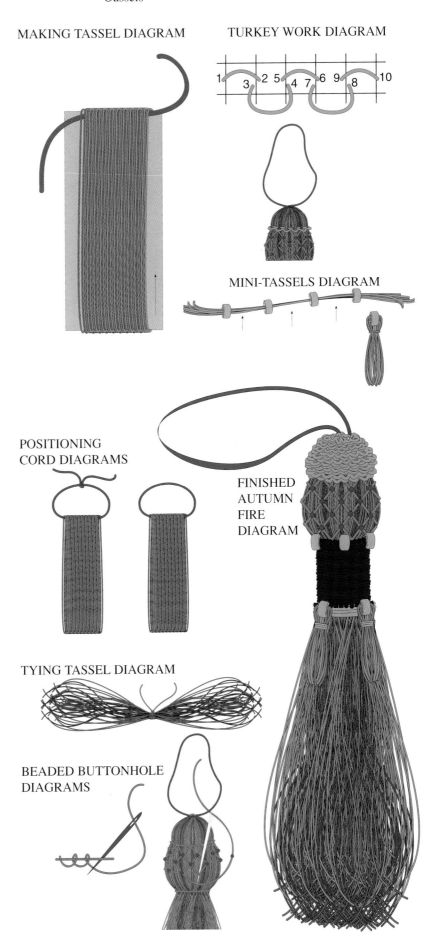

MAKING TASSEL DIAGRAM

TURKEY WORK DIAGRAM

MINI-TASSELS DIAGRAM

POSITIONING CORD DIAGRAMS

FINISHED AUTUMN FIRE DIAGRAM

TYING TASSEL DIAGRAM

BEADED BUTTONHOLE DIAGRAMS

$\mathcal{C}$ ATHERINE COLEMAN is presently residing in beautiful Sidney, British Columbia, Canada. Catherine has taught a wide variety of embroidery techniques, primarily canvas work, and has been involved in fiber art instruction for the last decade.

A graduate from the University of Alberta in home economics, she has taught throughout Canada and the United States. Her students give her rave reviews for her clear and concise stitch guides and her knowledge of finishing techniques, which she eagerly shares.

Her designs are widely distributed in the United States by Fleur de Paris Corporation. Catherine has been featured in *Needlepointers Magazine*, both the December 1994 and January 1995 issues of *McCall's Needlework Magazine* and *The Stitchery*.

She is a member of the Embroiderers' Guild of America, and the American Needlepoint Guild.

QUEEN GUINEVERE

Materials

Stretcher bars: 13" x 7"
Petit-point canvas #22 mesh: white (13" x 7")
DMC pearl cotton #12: white (3 balls)
DMC floss: white (1 skein)
Very fine braid #4: gold (15—10 m spools)
Bugle beads, 6 mm: white (2 packs)
Petite beads 12/0: gold (1 pack)
Fine braid #8: gold (9—10 m spools)
DMC Medicis: 478 white
Upholstery gimp, ¼": 50"
Wooden tassel base: 8½" (1)
Tapestry needle: #26
Beading needle
Tacky glue
Wet cloth
Loop turner
Rotary cutter
Cardboard (optional Plexiglas board) ¼": 24" x 6"

Directions

Use corresponding diagrams to work design.

1. Large Lower Band

Begin stitching at the center of stretcher bars, 1½" down from top outside edge of canvas. Using pearl cotton, stitch Small Crescent Heart Stitches (see page 48) and Double Leviathan Stitches (see page 20). Stitch a band that is three of the 4-part hearts, four of the 2-part hearts, and half of a 4-part heart at either end. The band's total length is 10½".

2. Large Lower Band

Stitch with very fine braid Star Eyelet Stitches inside 2-part hearts, Smyrna Cross-Stitches on either side of Double Leviathan Stitch, Cross-Stitches beside Star Eyelet Stitch, all Backstitches around hearts, and Four-Way Continental Stitches inside the 4-part hearts, Cross-Stitches on top of Double Leviathan and Backstitches on either side of it (see page 48 for "Star Eyelet Stitch," page 22 for "Smyrna Cross-Stitch," page 20 for "Cross-Stitch," page 20 for "Backstitch," and page 48 for "Four-Way Continental Stitch").

3. Large Lower Band

Stitch beads in place with 2-ply of DMC floss. Stitch each bead twice to secure (see page 20 for "Beading Stitch").

4. Large Lower Band

Tie down bugle beads with very fine braid. Backstitch on either side of Smyrna Cross-Stitches with pearl cotton. Backstitch around petite beads at corners with pearl cotton.

5. Small Upper Band

Stitch this piece 1" directly below Large Lower Band in the center of stretcher bars. With pearl cotton, stitch seven complete hearts and two half hearts at either end. The completed length is 6⅜".

6. Small Upper Band

With very fine braid, stitch Smyrna Cross-Stitches on either side of hearts. Backstitch around hearts. Stitch Star Eyelet Stitches and Cross-Stitches.

7. Small Upper Band

Stitch beads in place with DMC floss, 2-ply. Stitch twice to secure.

8. Small Upper Band

Tie down small bugle beads with very fine braid. Backstitch on either side of the Smyrna Cross-Stitches with pearl cotton.

Finishing Tassel

1. Prepare cording by dividing each 10 m spool of fine braid in four. Twist 4-ply in natural direction of fiber. Fold-twist in half, and let it twist back into itself to make a twisted ⅛" cording. Repeat for each spool to produce nine cords.

2. Push two wooden tassel base pieces together, connecting with small dowel piece.

3. Apply tacky glue to top and bottom flat sections where needlework will be placed. Allow glue to set up slightly so that it is tacky to the touch. Keep wet cloth nearby.

4. Trim needlework bands five threads away from finished work all around.

1. LARGE LOWER BAND DIAGRAM   **Each grid line = 1 thread**

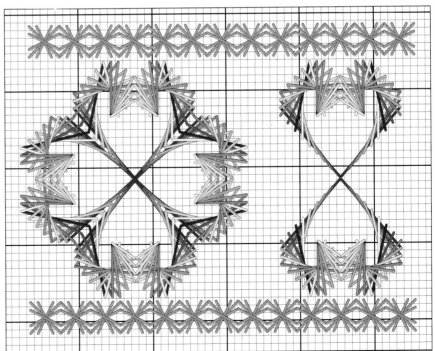

5. Wet needlework under the tap with cool water, and blot dry with a towel.

6. Place Small Upper Band at top flat section and Large Lower Band at lower flat section, one at a time, smoothing edges of canvas flat over curve of wood shape.

7. Where seams meet, apply gimp. Place a piece of cord on top of gimp, and secure with tacky glue. The Large Lower Band will require two pieces of gimp side by side to hide seam, with a piece of cord down the center of the two. Raw edges will be concealed later.

8. Insert loop turner at top of base through hole. Slide in all the way to the bottom. Loop one twisted cord into latch hook, and pull all the way through to the top, leaving a tail at the bottom which will be pinned and glued in place at the very bottom.

9. Apply tacky glue to wood base, from the very top to the point of meeting Small Upper Band of needlework. Allow it to become tacky. Apply cording all the way around wooden base top until meeting Small Upper Band.

10. Continue to apply cording to areas between needlework, all the way to the bottom of wooden base.

11. Apply gimp and cording with glue to the top at upper and lower edges of needlework.

2. LARGE LOWER BAND DIAGRAM

Each grid line = 1 thread

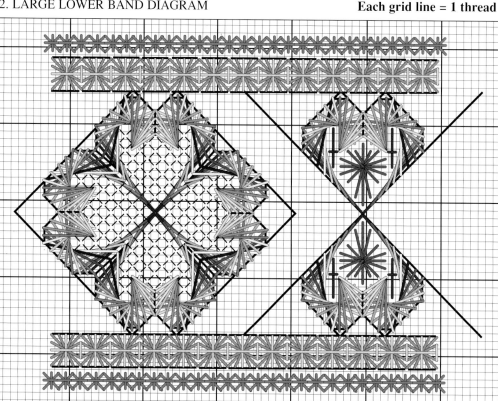

3. LARGE LOWER BAND DIAGRAM

Each grid line = 1 thread

12. Before beginning the skirt, wrap DMC Medicis in a ball, as this will prevent tangles.

13. Wrap DMC Medicis, pearl cotton, and very fine braid evenly around the cardboard, wrapping all three at once, from left to right, coming back from right to left with just pearl cotton and DMC Medicis.

14. With a threaded needle of pearl cotton, begin ¾" from top of skirt and tie together a group of threads about ¼" thick. Continue tying to make a continuous row of fringe for skirt. Repeat on back of board (see Queen Guinevere Skirt Diagram on page 48). When complete and secure, cut along lower edge of fringe with rotary cutter. Remove from board, and stitch back and front together to secure at point where both are tied.

15. Glue skirt onto lower edge of wooden base. There will be enough to wrap around twice. Glue gimp and cording on top of tie line.

16. Insert loop turner from top, and pull through cord for a hanger. Secure with several knots and bead of glue.

4. LARGE LOWER BAND DIAGRAM

Each grid line = 1 thread

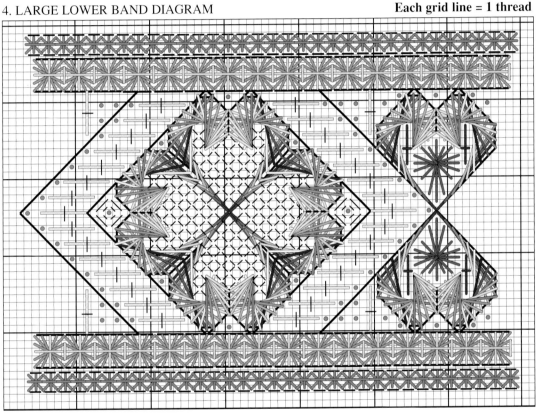

5. SMALL UPPER BAND DIAGRAM
Each grid line = 1 thread

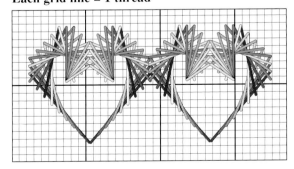

6. SMALL UPPER BAND DIAGRAM
Each grid line = 1 thread

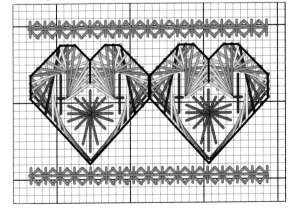

7. SMALL UPPER BAND DIAGRAM
Each grid line = 1 thread

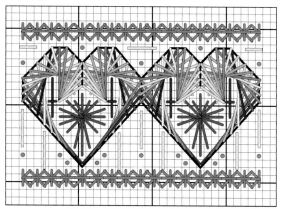

8. SMALL UPPER BAND DIAGRAM
Each grid line = 1 thread

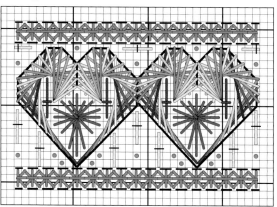

QUEEN GUINEVERE SKIRT DIAGRAM

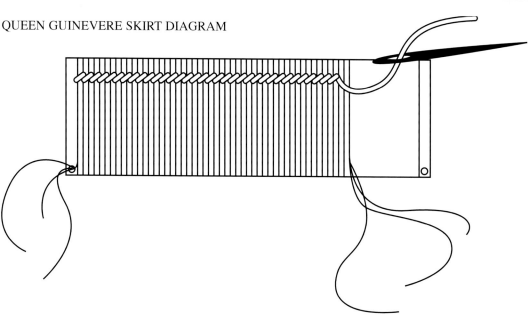

FOUR-WAY CONTINENTAL STITCH

This stitch is worked using small, diagonal Straight Stitches at specific intersections leading into the same hole. Follow diagram to determine sequence and direction of stitches.

STAR EYELET STITCH

This stitch consists of Straight Stitches radiating from the same center hole. Follow diagram sequence over required number of threads.

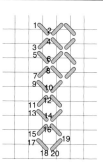

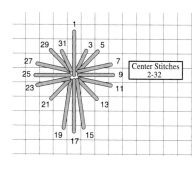

SMALL CRESCENT HEART STITCH

This stitch consists of long Satin Stitches overlapping each other around the curve of the shape. Follow the diagram sequence, coming up at 1, down at 2, and up at 3, finishing design.

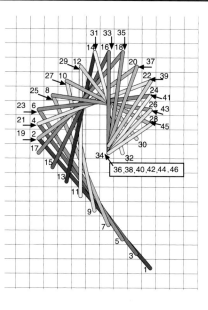

Surface Embroidery

S HAY PENDRAY has studied Japanese embroidery for 10 years with Master Saito in Japan and she was a driving force in bringing the art to the United States. She has recently traveled again to Japan to study with Kyoto Sensei, Koyo Kida. In turn, Shay shares her knowledge with the many students who she instructs in Japanese embroidery around the world.

BLUE & WHITE

Materials
Annebelle 28 ct.: white (10" square)
Anchor floss: 150 dk. blue, 120 lt. blue, 122 med. blue
Embroidery hoop
Crewel needle: #5 , #7
Dressmaker's carbon
Tracing paper

Directions
1. Begin by transferring design onto fabric (see page 53 for "Transferring").

2. The capital letters on the design refer to the color, and the numbers indicate the stitch to be used.

3. Using 1-ply of floss, stitch according to color and stitch key. Remember to stitch foreground areas first.

Color Key
A Anchor lt. blue
B Anchor med. blue
C Anchor dk. blue

Stitch Key
1 Darning Stitch (see page 57)
2 Cross-Stitch (see page 20)
3 Lattice Couching (see page 57)
4 Satin Stitch (see page 22)
5 Spike Stitch (see page 58)
6 French Knot (see page 21)
7 Outline Stitch (see page 58)
8 Chain Stitch (see page 57)
9 Herringbone Stitch (see page 21)
10 Straight Stitch (see page 37)

BLUE & WHITE DIAGRAM

*C*AROLYN HOOK was exposed to needlework at a very early age. As a child, she watched her mother sewing her clothes and tailoring her winter coat and hat, as well as embellishing some of her dresses with embroidery. Wanting to "do something too," Carolyn learned some embroidery stitches and stitched ever so diligently using her first hoop made from cardboard. Her enthusiasm for needlework never subsided. She continued under the tutelage of her mother and later explored and became self-taught in other aspects. She attended classes at the Elsa Williams School of Needle Art to fine-tune techniques and expand into other forms of needlework. Under the instruction of Shuji Tamura, Carolyn studied Japanese embroidery and graduated the ten phases in 1988. She continues to attend classes at the Japanese Embroidery Center in Georgia.

Seventeen years ago, Carolyn opened a needlework store and teaches several classes each week. She also has published *Fiber Fantasy, Second Edition* (as well as the first), which is a color comparison book for needlework threads on today's market. In addition, she has designed counted needlepoint, Hardanger patterns and crewel pieces, which are commercially available. She has found this form of art to be fulfilling, therapeutic and a satisfying release of creativity. In this day of "high tech," Carolyn hopes this art will pass on to our children so that they may pass it on to their children and keep it living for generations to come.

FLORAL IMPRESSIONS

Materials
Belgian linen (15" square)
Overdyed floss: shaded aqua, shaded brown
Lightweight Silk/Wool blend: green/ lavender/blue shades, jade green, lt. jade green, shaded jade green, pink, rose/purple shades, lt. yellow, yellow
Embroidery hoop
Crewel needles: #5 , #7
Dressmaker's carbon
Tracing paper

Notes
The use of a clean embroidery hoop is strongly suggested. Remove it from fabric when not stitching—even if only for a short period of time.

Overdyed floss is used in 3-ply, unless otherwise indicated on the design chart.

Stitch the foreground areas first, as each section is worked. This means that, when stitching a flower, for example, first work the petal that is completely exposed before stitching a petal that falls behind it. Do not use knots to begin and end threads.

Directions
1. Begin by transferring design onto fabric. First, place tracing paper over Floral Impressions Diagram and trace (see opposite page for "Transferring"). Do not trace the few flowers that are outlined in dots, as the stitches used may not cover the complete outline.

2. The capital letters on the diagram refer to the color, and the numbers indicate the stitch to be used.

3. Remember to stitch foreground areas first.

Special Instruction
Edging: Work outside edge of flower petals by making a row of small Split Stitches to give a nice smooth edge (see page 58 for "Split Stitch"). This also raises the edge a bit which can add some slight shading. This is a nice effect when smaller petals are left without edging. Remember this edging is only on the outside edge and not around entire shape.

Centers of pink flowers: Work with Overdyed floss 3-ply Buttonhole Stitch and Stem Stitch (see page 58 for "Buttonhole Stitch" and "Stem Stitch"). Be sure colors are aligned after stripping floss and putting strands back together.

Small round buds: Work Satin Stitch using different color sections from H to add variety. French Knots are colors J and K (see page 21 for "French Knots").

Tiny flowers: Work with overdyed floss, 2-ply, colors aligned. When Lazy Daisy Stitches are complete, do a Straight Stitch inside entire length of loop with same thread so that a different value of that thread is inside loop (see page 57 for "Lazy Daisy Stitch" and page 37 for "Straight Stitch"). This also adds dimension and shading to these little ones. Place a French Knot in center, using 3-ply overdyed floss color A (see page 21 for "French Knot").

Color Key
A Overdyed floss, shaded brown
B Overdyed floss, shaded aqua
C Lightweight Silk/Wool blend, pink
D Lightweight Silk/Wool blend, rose/purple shades
E Lightweight Silk/Wool blend, jade green
F Lightweight Silk/Wool blend, shaded jade green
G Lightweight Silk/Wool blend, lt. jade green
H Lightweight Silk/Wool blend, green/lavender/blue shades
J Lightweight Silk/Wool blend, lt. yellow
K Lightweight Silk/Wool blend, yellow

Stitch Key

1 Buttonhole Stitch (see page 58)
2 Stem Stitch (see page 58)
3 French Knot (see page 21)
4 Long and Short Stitch (see page 58)
5 Outline Stitch (see page 58)
6 Satin Stitch (see page 22)
7 Leaf Stitch (see page 57)
8 Fan Whipped Spider (see page 57)
9 Bullion Stitch (see page 20)
10 Lazy Daisy Stitch (see page 57)

Transferring

1. First, place tracing paper over the design and trace. Place fabric on a table or hard surface, and tape down corners and center of edge, making sure that fabric is smooth and won't slip. Place a piece of dressmaker's carbon down on the center of fabric with the proper side facing fabric (following manufacturer's instructions).

2. Place design tracing on top of carbon, and carefully pin both sheets of paper to the fabric. Trace over design tracing with a ballpoint pen that has run out of ink. Avoid using a pen or pencil that may puncture paper and put markings on fabric.

FLORAL IMPRESSIONS DIAGRAM

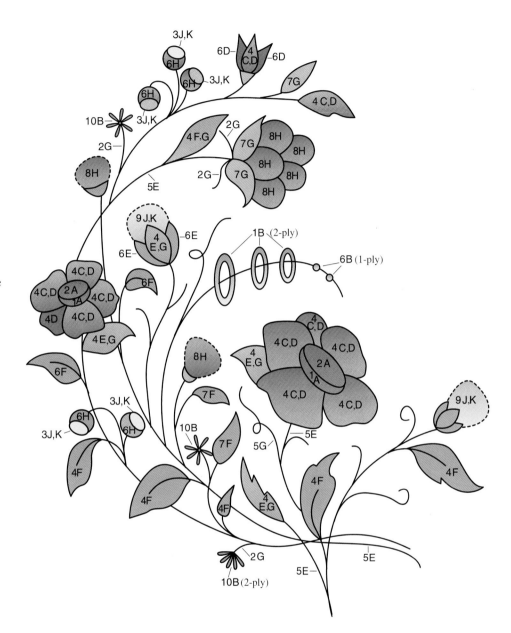

S UE LENTZ remembers always having a needle and thread of one sort or another in her hand. Her mother has pictures of Sue sitting under the sewing machine, fooling with fabric and thread at age three. Sue is still fooling with fabric and fiber, only now she shares her "foolings" with other stitchers.

Sue has been teaching count work for more than 20 years—the last 15 via the mail through *The Athelstane Stitcher's News*, a stitching newsletter from which she sells kits and instructions to her designs. She loves variety, so she uses lots of different fibers, colors, and stitches to create textured geometrics or other designs, borrowing inspiration from nature. Living on the Peshtigo River, in the woods of Northern Wisconsin, allows for lots of natural inspiration year-round.

In addition to designing and stitching, she also enjoys reading murder mysteries, gardening, and working out.

WINTER STAR

Stitched on glass blue Monaco 28, the finished design size is 8¼" x 6⅜". The fabric was cut 15" x 13" for the complete design.

The Winter Star Graph on page 56 shows only one-fourth of the completed design. Work the graph clockwise, turning one-quarter turn, until all four sides are completed.

Fabric	Design Size
Aida 11	20⅞" x 16⅜"
Aida 14	6⅜" x 12⅞"
Aida 18	12¾" x 10"
Hardanger 22	10½" x 8½"

Materials
Rayon thread for needlepoint 18 ct.: white
Kid Mohair & Nylon: white
Tubular Nylon Netting: white
Blending Filament: pearl, rainbow
Very fine #4 cord: gold
Anchor pearl cotton #8: white
Beads: 2½ mm silver (20), medium bugle (8)

Directions
Use corresponding section numbers provided on Winter Star Graph on page 56 to work design.

Section 1
Work center motif with two strands rayon thread (dampened and separated) Satin Stitch (see page 22 for "Satin Stitch").

Section 2
Work diamond area using one strand pearl cotton Oblong Cross-Stitch (see page 58 for "Oblong Cross-Stitch").

Section 3
Work leaves with one strand very fine cord Mini-Leaf Stitch (see page 58 for "Mini-Leaf Stitch").

Section 4
Work diamond border with one strand very fine cord in Double Running Stitch (see page 57 for "Double Running Stitch").

Section 5
Continue outward outlining star, using one strand tubular netting Satin Stitch.

Section 6
Work next row (inner row) with one strand pearl cotton Satin Stitch.

Section 7
Work floating snowflakes with one strand kid mohair & nylon Star Stitch (see page 58 for "Star Stitch").

Section 8
Work Square Rhodes Stitch and Diamond Rhodes Stitch with one strand pearl blending filament with one strand rainbow blending filament (see page 58 for "Square Rhodes Stitch" and page 57 for "Diamond Rhodes Stitch").

Section 9
Work Mini Kloster Blocks with two strands pearl blending filament and two strands rainbow blending filament (see page 58 for "Mini Kloster Blocks").

Section 10
Sew 2½ mm silver beads in center of each kid mohair & nylon star and each of the pearl cotton motifs stitched in the diamond area (see page 20 for "Beading Stitch").

Section 11
On the very center of the piece, use eight bugle beads to form a star pattern covering seams.

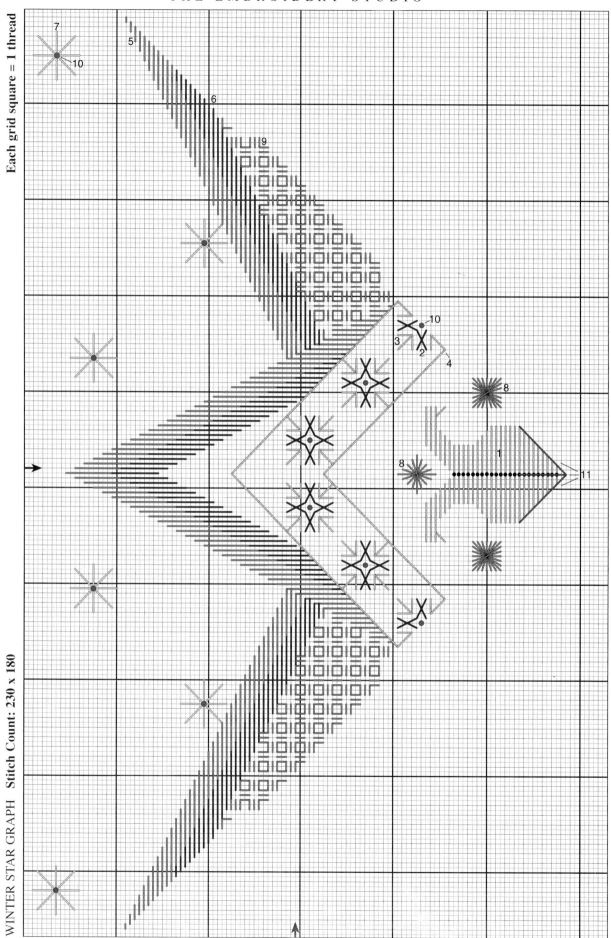

Each grid square = 1 thread

WINTER STAR GRAPH   Stitch Count: 230 x 180

CHAIN STITCH

Bring needle up at 1. Keep the thread flat, untwisted and full. Put the needle down through fabric at 2 and back up through at 3, keeping the thread under the needle to form a loop. Pull the thread through, leaving the loop loose and full. To form the next chain loop which holds the previous one in place, go down at 4 and back up at 5. Continue to form each chain loop in the same manner. Finish with a short Straight Stitch over the bottom of the last loop to secure in place.

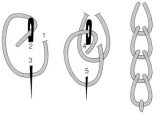

DARNING STITCH

This stitch is worked in lines using continuous Straight Stitches that aren't very long with very little space between them. These stitches can be vertical, horizontal, diagonal, or curved to follow the outline.

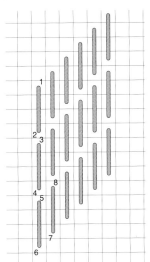

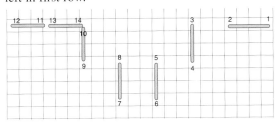

DIAMOND RHODES STITCH

Stitch a vertical Straight Stitch over nine horizontal threads, coming up at 1 and down at 2. Bring needle back up at 3 (one thread over and one thread up from the bottom left). Insert needle at 4 (one thread over and one thread down from the top right). Continue working stitches to 10. Bring needle up at 11 (one thread up and over from 9). Insert needle at 12 (one thread down and over from 10). Continue to 16.

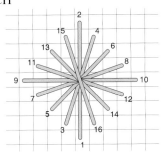

DOUBLE RUNNING STITCH

Working from right to left, work Running Stitches over and under three threads of fabric, following shape to be stitched. Work back from left to right, filling in the spaces left in first row.

FAN WHIPPED SPIDER

Working from right to left, stitch spokes in shape to be worked. Bring needle up at narrowest portion of shape outside of the first spoke. Pass needle under the first spoke. Go back over the first spoke, and pass needle under the next two spokes. Continue going back over one spoke and passing forward under two spokes. At the end of the row, go under only one spoke and go down with the needle on outside of shape. Run needle under Straight Stitches on back, and carry to right side. Continue for next row, pushing back stitches from previous row.

LATTICE COUCHING STITCH

This stitch consists of horizontal and vertical Straight Stitches worked at even intervals to form a grid. The intersections are then crossed with small diagonal Straight Stitches in one direction only.

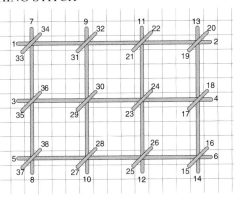

LAZY DAISY STITCH

Bring the needle up at 1. Keep the thread flat, untwisted and full. Put the needle down through fabric at 2 and up through at 3, keeping the thread under the needle to form a loop. Pull the thread through, leaving the loop loose and full. To hold the loop in place, go down on other side of thread near 3, forming a Straight Stitch over loop.

LEAF STITCH

For tip of leaf, make a small Straight Stitch (1). Make slanted Straight Stitches from side to side to fill leaf (2).

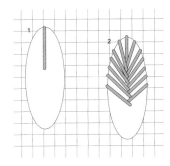

LONG AND SHORT STITCH

Work the foundation row, alternating long and short Satin Stitches, following the contours of the shape to be filled. Keep stitches close together so that fabric is not visible. On the next row, fit stitches of equal length into spaces left by short stitches in previous row. Continue until shape is filled.

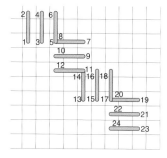

MINI KLOSTER BLOCKS

Smaller than Kloster Blocks, these consist of three Satin Stitches worked over two threads.

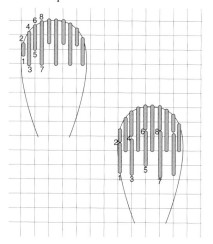

MINI-LEAF STITCH

Work this stitch using three Straight Stitches. Follow sequence in diagram, inserting needle at the same point on each down stitch.

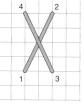

OBLONG CROSS-STITCH

This stitch is an elongated version of the Cross-Stitch. Bring needle up at lower right-hand side. Insert needle up four threads and over two threads. Continue working diagonal Straight Stitches across row. Pass back over row and work other half of crosses. Stitch remaining rows, working in same directions as first.

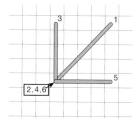

OUTLINE STITCH

Bring the needle out at the end of the line at 1. Keep the thread to the right and above the needle. Push needle down at 2 and back up at 3.

SPIKE STITCH or BUTTONHOLE STITCH

Bring needle up at 1, go down at 2, and come up at 3, looping thread under needle. Continue for length of stitch, keeping needle vertical. For Spike Stitch, the "spikes" point away from the body of the design.

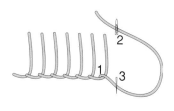

SPLIT STITCH

Come up at 1, and go down at 2. Split the stitch in the middle, as the needle comes out at 3, and go down at 4. Repeat to fill area.

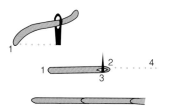

SQUARE RHODES STITCH

Bring the thread through at 1, and down at 2, up at 3, down at 4. Continue in this manner, following the direction of the numbering, each stitch overlapping the previous, until the square is filled.

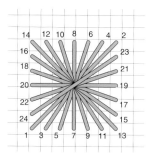

STAR STITCH

Bring needle up at 1, down at 2, up at 3, down at 4, and up at 5. Continue around until eight stitches have been made, all coming down into the center. Note the longer vertical and horizontal stitches.

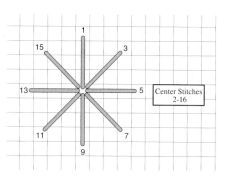

STEM STITCH

Bring the needle out at the end of the line at 1. Keep the thread to the right and below the needle. Push needle down at 2 and back up at 3.

Counted Cross-Stitch

HOME SWEET HOME

Stitched on antique white Cashel linen 28 over 2 threads, the finished design size is 14⅛" x 14⅛". The fabric was cut 21" x 21". See Index for stitches.

Fabric	Design Size
Aida 11	18" x 18"
Aida 18	11" x 11"
Hardanger 22	9" x 9"

THE VANESSA-ANN Collection has been, for more than 15 years, in the forefront of the needlework and craft industry. Working from offices in Ogden, Utah, the Vanessa-Ann staff is busy designing, packaging, and producing about 20 books per year.

Although best known for cross-stitch books, The Vanessa-Ann Collection, under the name, "Chapelle Limited," has crossed over into almost every craft imaginable, from juggling to woodworking, rubber stamping to quilting, knot tying to music boxes.

A staff of 20 employees, as well as many out-of-house designers, crafters, and stitchers, spend their days planning, painting, sewing, building, researching, editing, and photographing projects for upcoming books.

With so much diversity within a company, there must be an effective leader. Such is the case with Vanessa-Ann's president, Jo Packham. With so many ideas swimming around in her head, there is never a shortage of projects for the staff designers to create.

A native of Ogden, Jo attended the University of Utah for two years and graduated from California State University at Sacramento in art and child development. She loves spending time with her family, decorating, shopping, and dreaming up new ideas for her company.

Anchor   DMC

Step 1: Cross-Stitch (2 strands)

Anchor		DMC	
301		744	Yellow–pale
890		729	Old Gold–med.
332		946	Burnt Orange–med.
47		321	Christmas Red
98		553	Violet–med.
210	E	562	Jade–med.
212		561	Jade–vy. dk.
242		989	Forest Green
244		987	Forest Green–dk.
216	N	367	Pistachio Green–dk.
879		890	Pistachio Green–ultra dk.
403	Z	310	Black

Step 2: Cross-Stitch (1 strand)

879		890	Pistachio Green–ultra dk.
860		3053	Green Gray
846		3051	Green Gray–dk.

Step 3: Queen Stitch (2 strands)

301		744	Yellow–pale
890		729	Old Gold–med.
47		321	Christmas Red
43		815	Garnet–med.
95		554	Violet–lt.
98		553	Violet–med.

Step 4: Long & Short Stitch (2 strands)

890		729	Old Gold–med.
332		946	Burnt Orange–med.
47		321	Christmas Red
43		815	Garnet–med.

Step 5: Star Stitch (6 strands)

121		794	Cornflower Blue–lt. (bottom star)
162		517	Wedgwood–dk. (top cross)
121		517	Wedgwood–dk. (bottom star)
162		794	Cornflower Blue–lt. (top cross)

Step 6: Chain Stitch (1 strand)

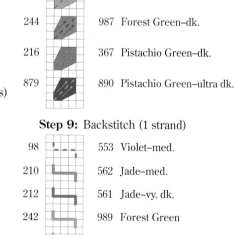

95		554	Violet–lt.
846		3051	Green Gray–dk.

Step 7: Long Stitch (3 strands)

890		729	Old Gold–med.
332		946	Burnt Orange–med.
244		987	Forest Green–dk. (2 strands)
216		367	Pistachio Green–dk. (2 strands)

Step 8: Satin Stitch (2 strands)

301		744	Yellow–pale
95		554	Violet–lt.
98		553	Violet–med.
210		562	Jade–med.
212		561	Jade–vy. dk.
242		989	Forest Green
244		987	Forest Green–dk.
216		367	Pistachio Green–dk.
879		890	Pistachio Green–ultra dk.

Step 9: Backstitch (1 strand)

98		553	Violet–med.
210		562	Jade–med.
212		561	Jade–vy. dk.
242		989	Forest Green

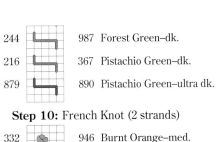

244		987	Forest Green–dk.
216		367	Pistachio Green–dk.
879		890	Pistachio Green–ultra dk.

Step 10: French Knot (2 strands)

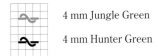

332		946	Burnt Orange–med.
43		815	Garnet–med.
98		553	Violet–med.
403		310	Black

Step 11: Beading Stitch

	Seed 11/0	Pale Yellow
	Seed 11/0	Pink
	Seed 11/0	Blue

Silk Ribbon

Step 1: Whipped Running Stitch

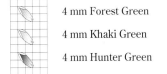

4 mm Jungle Green

4 mm Hunter Green

Step 2: Fly Stitch

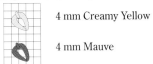

4 mm Forest Green

Step 3: Japanese Ribbon Stitch

4 mm Forest Green

4 mm Khaki Green

4 mm Hunter Green

Step 4: Lazy Daisy Stitch

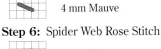

4 mm Creamy Yellow

4 mm Mauve

Step 5: Straight Stitch

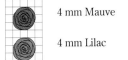

4 mm Mauve

Step 6: Spider Web Rose Stitch

4 mm Mauve

4 mm Lilac

Step 7: French Knot

4 mm Creamy Yellow

4 mm Mauve

HOME SWEET HOME TOP LEFT **Stitch Count: 199 x 199**
Each grid square = 2 threads

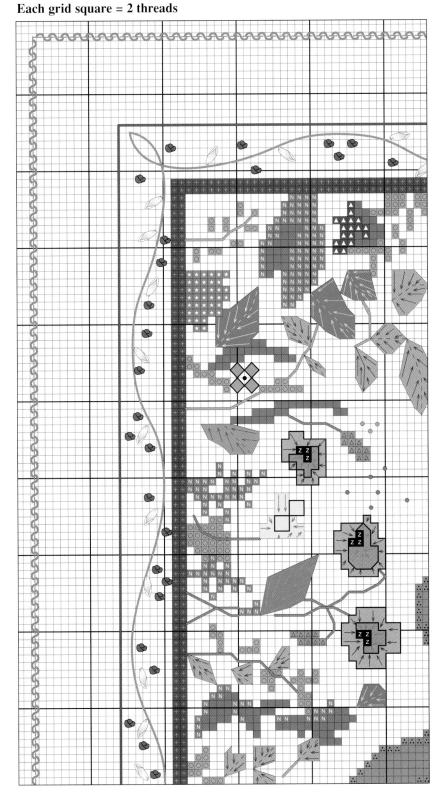

HOME SWEET HOME TOP MIDDLE

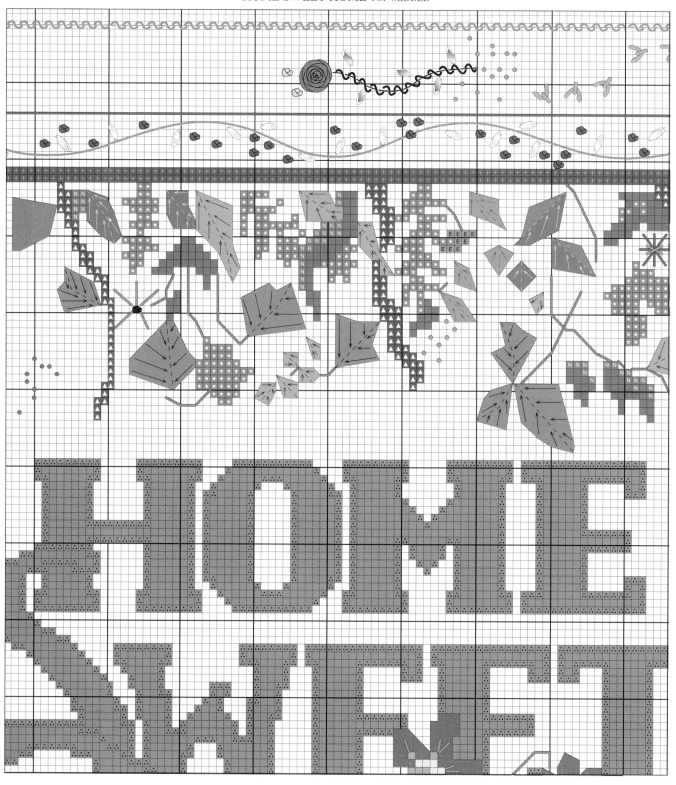

HOME SWEET HOME TOP RIGHT

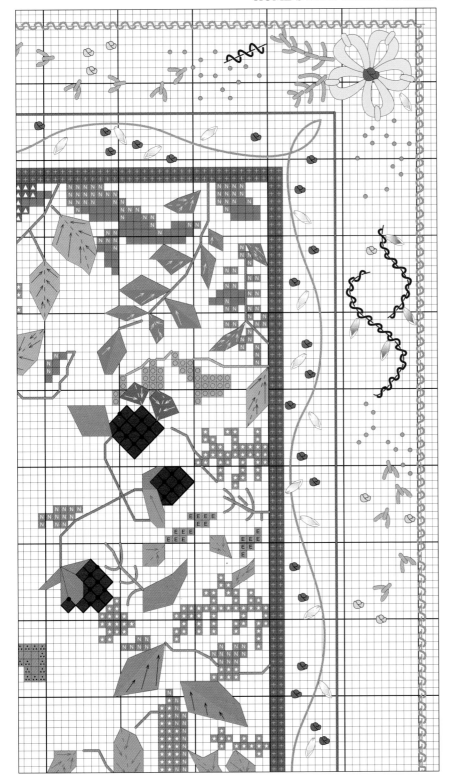

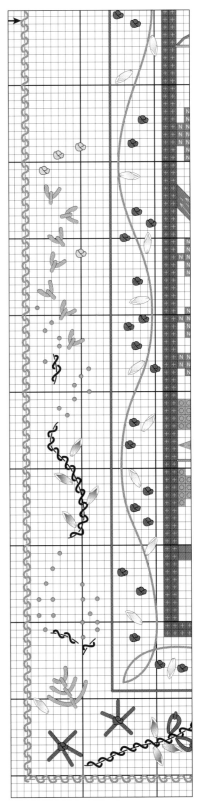

HOME SWEET HOME
BOTTOM LEFT

HOME SWEET HOME BOTTOM MIDDLE

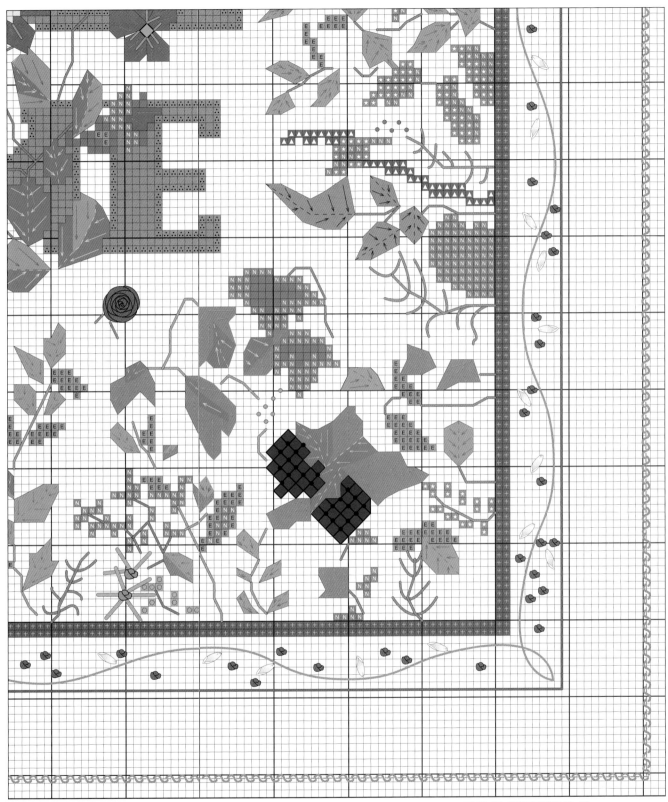

HOME SWEET HOME BOTTOM RIGHT

VICKI HASTINGS thinks of life as vegetable soup, slow simmered and with a contemplative flavor. For ingredients, there are the vast variety of life experiences one adds over time.

Her personal soup recipe began as clam chowder. She grew up collecting shells and walking the Atlantic shore on the New Jersey coast. The broth of these early years has proven rich and sustaining. She loved every ingredient, from the schools she attended—especially her incredible art teacher—to the hurricanes and winter storms.

As she entered college, her family moved to South Dakota. Clam chowder now became beef stew—the hearty, stick-to-your-ribs variety. She began studying art, but, after a year, changed her major to English literature. She has always found it difficult to choose between pictures that tell a story and words that paint pictures.

In school, she met her husband, Bob. They have moved the family kettle around the country. They are presently living in St. Louis.

Vicki and Bob have three children. Scott is a graduate student at St. Andrews University in Scotland, Kelly is a graduate student at the University of Alaska, and Heather is a high school junior and prospective art student.

Twelve years ago they added an interesting flavor called the Cross-Eyed Cricket to this "soup of life." Vicki, Bob, and their partners, Nickie and Jimmy Odom, create and sell needlework designs under the name, The Cricket Collection.

What will be the next ingredient? It is the element of surprise that keeps the flavor so intriguing. "And, after all," says Vicki. "Life is a recipe in

COUNTING SHEEP

Stitched on wild honey Heatherfield 10, the finished design size is 8¼" x 8¼". The fabric was cut 14" x 14". See Index for stitches.

Fabric	Design Size
Aida 11	7½" x 7½"
Aida 14	5⅞" x 5⅞"
Aida 18	4½" x 4⅝"
Hardanger 22	3¾" x 3¾"

Anchor   DMC

Step 1: Cross-Stitch (4 strands)

Anchor		DMC	
72	■	902	Garnet–vy.dk.
189		991	Aquamarine–dk.
842		3013	Khaki Green–lt.
845	◎	3011	Khaki Green–dk.
8581		3023	Brown Gray–lt.
387	·	822	Beige Gray–lt.
830		644	Beige Gray–med.
392		642	Beige Gray–dk.
401		844	Beaver Gray–ultra dk.
403	■	310	Black

Step 2: Backstitch (2 strands)

246	⌐	895	Christmas Green–dk.
401	⌐	844	Beaver Gray–ultra dk.

Step 3: Beading Stitch

◎ Craft bell 9 mm

COUNTING SHEEP   Stitch Count: 82 x 83   **Each grid square = 1 stitch**

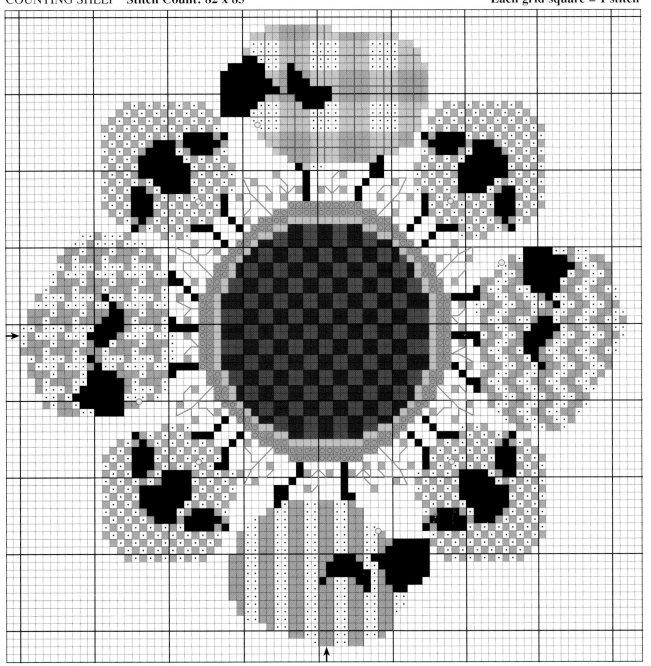

*C*AROLYN MEACHAM is a needlework designer and teacher who specializes in counted-thread techniques. She has been embroidering since she was five years old and combined a passionate love of all needlearts with an art background to create a career.

Twenty years ago, she and her husband, Mike, started Serendipity Designs, a needlework publishing company. Today they manufacture a wide variety of needlework kits and accessories that are sold throughout the world. They also founded Charted Designers of America and are actively involved in promoting the needlework industry and embroidery education.

Carolyn is best known for her classic floral and Oriental cross-stitch designs which are usually done on a grand scale. Canvas stitchery, however, is her favorite technique, and she is currently working on a book of Florentine patterns for a British publisher. She has studied extensively, both locally and abroad, and her designs have won several international awards. She is an avid collector of antique sewing tools and, in addition to her stitchery, loves to travel, read, and cook.

UNDERWATER FANTASY

Stitched on delft blue Rebecca 22 over 2, the finished design size is 8⅛" x 9⅞". The fabric was cut 15" x 16". See Index for stitches.

Fabric	Design Size
Aida 14	6⅜" x 7¼"
Aida 18	5" x 6"
Hardanger 22	4⅛" x 4⅞"

Anchor		DMC	

Step 1: Cross-Stitch (3 strands)

1	· /		White
926			Ecru
933		543	Beige Brown–ultra vy. lt.
292	○	3078	Golden Yellow–vy. lt.
293		727	Topaz–vy. lt.
295	∴	726	Topaz–lt.
297	★	743	Yellow–med. (2 strands)
295		726	Topaz–lt. (1 strand)
1002		977	Golden Brown–lt.
1003	E ◢	721	Orange Spice–med.
10		352	Coral–lt. (2 strands)
9		353	Peach (1 strand)
11		350	Coral–med. (2 strands)
10		352	Coral–lt. (1 strand)
1038		519	Sky Blue (2 strands)
433		996	Electric Blue–med. (1 strand)
1039		518	Wedgwood–lt. (2 strands)
433		996	Electric Blue–med. (1 strand)
433		996	Electric Blue–med. (2 strands)
1039	N N	518	Wedgwood–lt. (1 strand)
886	U	3047	Yellow Beige–lt.
887		372	Mustard–lt.
831		642	Beige Gray–dk. (2 strands)
378		841	Beige Brown–lt. (1 strand)
399		318	Steel Gray–lt.
235	H	414	Steel Gray–dk.
400		317	Pewter Gray (2 strands)
235		414	Steel Gray–dk. (1 strand)
403	K ◣	310	Black

Step 2: Backstitch (3 strands)

433		996	Electric Blue–med.
403		310	Black
235		414	Steel Gray–dk. (1 strand)

Step 3: French Knot (1 strand)

1		White

Step 4: Darning Stitch (1 strand)

Blending filament Blue metallic

Step 5: Tacked Ribbon Stitch

Silk ribbon 4 mm Green

Step 6: Beading Stitch

●	Pearl 3 mm
●	Pearl 4 mm
●	Pearl 5 mm
●	Pearl 6 mm

Step 7: Attaching Seashells

Seashells (see photo)

ATTACHING SEASHELLS

Tack shell down with two stitches over base bar of shell. Stitch over remaining three sides of shell by bringing needle up at 1, down at 2, up at 3, and down at 4. Come up at 5, wrap around first thread, wrap around second thread, and go down at 6. Come up at 2, wrap around first thread, wrap around second thread, and go down at 4.

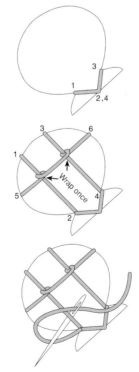

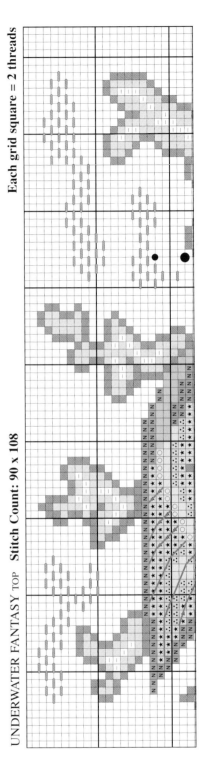

Each grid square = 2 threads

Stitch Count: 90 x 108

UNDERWATER FANTASY TOP

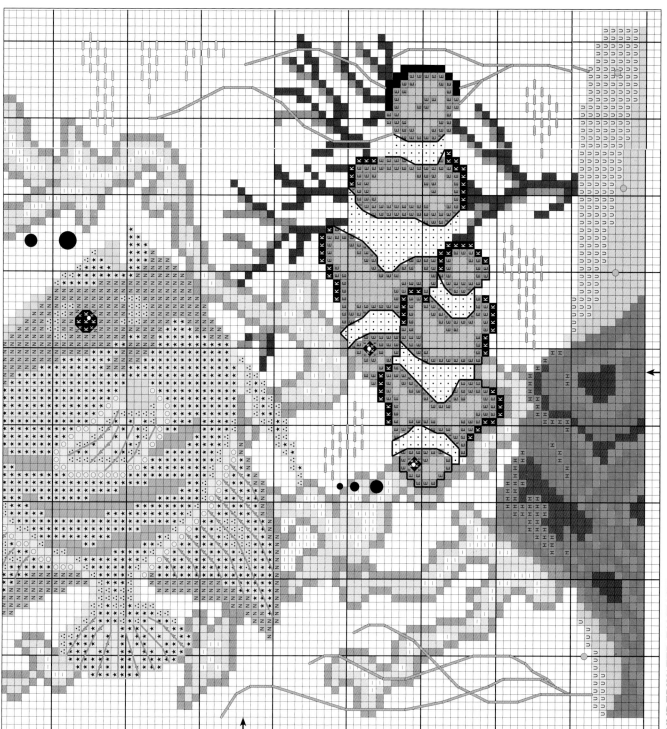

UNDERWATER FANTASY BOTTOM

CHAIN ROSE

Work Chain Stitch in a spiral manner (see page 57 for "Chain Stitch"). For rose, start the chain in the center, working in a tight spiral. Gradually increase the size of the spiral as you work toward the outer edge of the rose. Finish with a short Straight Stitch over the bottom of the last loop to secure in place.

FLY STITCH

Bring the needle up at 1. Keep the thread flat, untwisted, and full. Put the needle down through the fabric at 2 and up at 3, keeping the thread under the needle forming a "U". Pull the thread through, leaving the drape loose and full. To hold the thread in place, go down on other side of thread at 4, forming a Straight Stitch over loop. The length of the Straight Stitch may vary according to the desired effect.

JAPANESE RIBBON STITCH

Come up through fabric at the starting point of stitch. Lay the ribbon flat on the fabric. At the end of the stitch, pierce the ribbon with the needle. Slowly pull the length of the ribbon through to the back, allowing the ends of the ribbon to curl. If the ribbon is pulled too tight, the effect of the stitch can be lost. Vary the petals and leaves by adjusting the length, the tension of the ribbon before piercing, the position of piercing, and how loosely or tightly the ribbon is pulled down through itself.

QUEEN STITCH

This stitch consists of a group of four vertical stitches worked into the same space. Each is crossed with a small horizontal stitch.

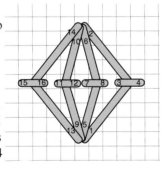

Come up at 1, down at 2, and up just to the right at 3. Cross the stitch and come down at 4 and back up at 5.

Continue until all four stitches have been worked and crossed. Come back up at the bottom of where the next stitch will be worked. This stitch works best when rows are done diagonally.

SPIDER WEB ROSE

Using two strands of floss, securely work Straight Stitches to form five spokes (1). These are anchor stitches to create the rose with ribbon.

Bring the piece of ribbon up through the center of the spokes (2). Weave the ribbon over one spoke and under the next spoke, continuing around in one direction (clockwise or counterclockwise), until the spokes are covered (3,4 and 5). When weaving, keep ribbon loose and allow to twist.

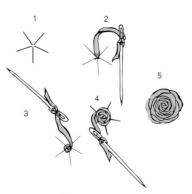

STAR FILLING STITCH

Following numbering on diagram, work an upright Cross-Stitch. Work a Cross-Stitch on top. This may be done in a different color. Work an Oblong Cross-Stitch on the top of both to finish the stitch.

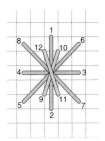

TACKED RIBBON

Using one needle threaded with embroidery floss, come up under the silk ribbon which is lying flat on the fabric.

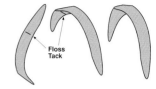

Tack the ribbon in place; come up again at desired interval and tack. To turn the ribbon flow in another direction, tack the ribbon with the floss from underneath and fold the ribbon over the floss.

WHIPPED RUNNING STITCH

Complete the Running Stitches first. Come up at 1 and go down at 2. Come up at 3, allowing an unstitched space between stitches. Continue with next stitch in the same manner as 1–2.

To whip the running stitch, go under the first Running Stitch from 1 to 2. (Be careful not to pierce the fabric or catch the Running Stitch.) Come up on the other side of the stitch. Keeping the thread flat, wrap over the stitch and go under the next Running Stitch at 3, and then at 4. Continue in the same manner. The effect can be varied by how loosely or tightly the thread is pulled when whipping.

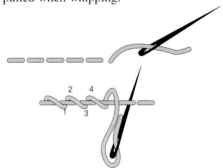

$\mathcal{J}$UDY BISHOP'S talent for artistic clothing evolves from a varied background, which includes college instructor of fashion design, business entrepreneur, and designer of Art-to-Wear clothing. With a B.S. in education from Missouri University, she completed her master's degree in home economics, specializing in clothing and textiles, at California State University, Long Beach.

Her one-of-a-kind garments have received awards and been shown at exhibitions throughout the United States, including New York's Tenth Biennial Exhibition of The Embroiderers' Guild of America (EGA), The Twelfth and Thirteenth National Exhibit of EGA, "Stitch in Time" Fashion Show at the International Quilt Festival in Houston, Texas, the Colorado Gallery of Arts' "Art To Wear" Fashion Exhibit, American Quilter's Society Juried Fashion Shows, and Fairfield's Invitational Royal Star Fashion Show. In 1996, her garments will be displayed in the Invitational Fashion Show sponsored by Hobbs Bonded Fiber for Australia's first Quilt Market and Show.

In 1992, Judy was featured as one of the Designers Across America in *Needlearts* magazine. In 1993, she was accepted into Fiber Forum, a juried group of fiber artists organized to further the advancement of needle-work as an art form. She developed a group correspondence course for the Embroiderers' Guild of America, introducing members to the basics as they create contemporary pieces.

Combining her knowledge of needle-art techniques and her love of textiles, Judy has worked with such fabric companies as P&B Textiles, John Kaldor Fabricmaker, Cherry-wood Hand-dyed Fabrics, Inc., and Mission Valley Textiles, to design and create garments to introduce their new fabric collections at various industry shows.

As a teacher/lecturer, Judy encourages students to think of clothing in a new way. Emphasis is placed on the concept that embellished garment designs should enhance the human body. Her goal in teaching is to provide students with the knowledge and encouragement to create functional artistic clothing.

Judy has used her 35 years of sewing experience together with 23 years of teaching to launch her new garment pattern line, From the Judy Bishop Collection. Devoting herself, full time, to her business, Judy Bishop Designs, she continues to travel, giving lectures and workshops on wearable art.

VICTORIAN PATCHWORK VEST

Materials

Fine-quality muslin: 1 yd. (for piecing
    foundation and underlining)
Assorted cotton solids: lt., med., and
    dk. values, ¼ yd. each (10)
Coordinating solid fabric: 1 yd. (for
    vest back, front sides, front band)
Lining fabric: 1 yd.
Tricot fusible interfacing: ¾ yd.
Rotary cutter and mat
Ruler
Pearl cotton thread #8: black
Beading thread
Piping: 3 yds. (optional)
Indian seed beads: black
Chalk marker, washable
Needles: #7 crewel, #8 sharp
Iron
Scissors: fabric and small pointed
Soft terry cloth for pressing
Straight pins

Notes

Yardage amounts are given for a
medium-size vest using a pattern by
this designer. When using other
garment patterns, check instructions to
determine fabric amounts needed. To
order pattern used, write to Chapelle
Limited, Inc.

When making garment, construct a test
sample to ensure that garment fits
before beginning the project. Make any
pattern alterations at this time.

Directions

1. Pretreat assorted solid cotton fabrics
by washing in cool water and drying on
low heat. Press to remove wrinkles.

2. Cut out front pattern pieces from
muslin foundation.

3. Piece patchwork onto muslin
foundation. Complete one front and
then lay second muslin front beside it.
Use first front as a guide to achieve
balanced color placement.

Guidelines for Piecing

• Use a ¼" seam allowance when
piecing.
• Press each strip after it has been
flipped.
• When next strip is added, it could be
placed at an angle from raw edge to
form a more interesting design or form
a continuous line after it has been
flipped. To check, insert straight pins
parallel to raw edge and flip strip over.
• Watch placement of the colors to
ensure a good balance of color.

Use rotary cutter, mat, and ruler to cut
a strip 3 to 3½" wide from each of the
10 solid fabrics. Cut additional strips as
needed.

Cut an irregular shape, either 3, 4, or 5
sided, as a center focal point (see page
74 for Center Focal Point Pattern
Diagrams). Place right side up on
muslin foundation. Begin in a
clockwise direction to add a strip to
each side. Place right side of cut strip
against right side of center shape (see
page 75 for Piecing Fabric Strips
Diagram). Flip fabric strip so that right
side is facing up.

Following same procedure, add another
fabric strip to cover raw edges of center
shape and first strip. Continue working
around entire center shape, covering
raw edges. Once raw edges of center
shape have been covered, lift up strips
and cut away excess fabric from
underneath. Continue adding fabric
strips to raw edges, and cover entire
muslin foundation (see page 75 for
Covering Foundation Diagram).

An alternate way of piecing is to sew
several strips together in an angular
manner and cut out a wedge shape (see
page 74 for Pieced Wedge Diagram).
Place right sides of pieced wedge along
raw edge of attached fabric strip and
sew to the foundation (see page 75 for
Covering Foundation Diagram #8). Flip

wedge and press seam. If fabric strips
extend beyond muslin foundation, cut
off excess.

When patchwork is complete, lay front
pattern piece on top of piece panels to
compare shapes. Trim away any excess
fabric. Machine-baste ⅜" from raw
edges to hold layers together and to
stabilize cut edges in preparation for
surface embroidery.

4. Start surface embroidery. *Note:*
Before beginning to stitch, use a
washable chalk pencil to mark seam
line around all outside edges. These
drawn lines will be used as a guide to
begin and end stitches a scant ⅛" away
to avoid being caught during
construction of finished product.

Stitch embroidery patterns. Embroidery
Fronts Diagram can be used as pattern
for stitching (see page 75). Patterns are
organized according to foundation
stitch used. The overall look will
vary— tall, short, open, dense, lacy,
geometric. Try to vary stitch placement
to avoid having similar patterns next to
each other. Place an elaborate stitch
pattern next to a simple one, a
geometric pattern next to a curvilinear
one. Simple stitch patterns can act as
fillers (see pages 82 to 84 for Crazy
Quilt stitches).

When stitching second front, the same
stitches could be used but placed in
different locations.

5. Add beads to project (see page 20
for "Beading Stitch"). Use a strong
beading thread when attaching beads.

Complete beading for one front, and
use it as a guide when attaching beads
on second front to achieve balance.

6. When surface embroidery and
beading have been completed, place a
soft terry towel on ironing board. Lay
right side of the embellished panel
against towel and lightly press.

7. Construction of garment. Cut out
front and back sides from coordinating
solid fabric. Use muslin as an

underlining on these garment pattern pieces to maintain same weight as pieced sections. Otherwise, garment will not hang properly. Cut underlining pieces from muslin, using same pattern pieces used to cut out fashion fabric. Place muslin to wrong side of fashion fabric, and treat the two as one during construction.

8. The optional piping should be applied along seam lines of garment sections that will be sewn to pieced panels, such as front side sections and front band.

9. Construct garment, following pattern instructions. Press seams open, except along pieced panels. These seams should be pressed toward unpieced solid sections to avoid bulky seams. Use lightweight fusible interfacing on the front band to provide support.

CENTER FOCAL POINT PATTERN DIAGRAMS **Enlarge 150%**—seam allowance included

PIECED WEDGE DIAGRAM   **Enlarge to 125%**—Seam allowance included.

Place along Outside Edge

Dotted lines indicate pieced seams

Top

Bottom

Front Edge

PIECING FABRIC STRIPS DIAGRAM

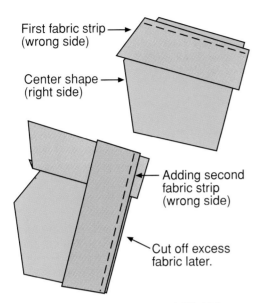

First fabric strip (wrong side)

Center shape (right side)

Adding second fabric strip (wrong side)

Cut off excess fabric later.

COVERING FOUNDATION DIAGRAM

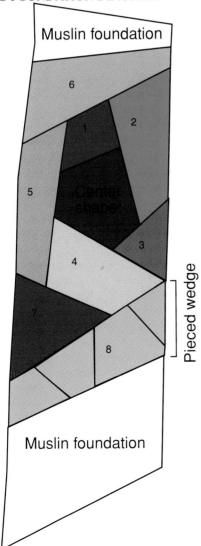

Muslin foundation

6

1

2

5

Center shape

4

3

7

8

Pieced wedge

Muslin foundation

EMBROIDERY FRONTS DIAGRAM

Pieced wedge

Pieced wedge

"REFLECTING ON MY LIFE, I realize needlework has played a large part in my personal development," says Deanna Powell.

Deanna has been designing needlework, embellished clothing, and accessories since 1977 and teaching quilt design and technique since 1978. The quiltmaking phase of her career complements her many years of teaching needlearts and offers her students the opportunity to combine quilting with other embroidery techniques. She has taught at The Embroiderers' Guild of America (EGA) national and regional seminars, Callaway School of Needle Arts, National Academy of Needlearts, National Quilt Association, American Quilt Society, and quilting seminars, as well as chapters, shops, and guilds. Additionally, Deanna is a charter member of Fiber Forum, an EGA group formed to advance the perception of needlework as an art form. She is an EGA certified teacher in quiltmaking, certified graduate teacher, and current vice president of operations for EGA. To share her knowledge, she has contributed to quilt magazines and has self-published several booklets and numerous patterns.

SOFT CASE

Materials

Faille: ecru or black (12" x 25")
Muslin: (12" x 25")
Sewing thread: pastel color
Dressmaker's carbon
Tracing wheel (optional)
8" quilting hoop
Pearl cotton #8: assorted colors
Metal thread: assorted colors
Silk thread: assorted colors
Rayon thread: assorted colors
Needles (appropriate for fibers used)
Batting: lightweight (8" x 20¼"),
  (8" x 12") for inner pocket, (¼ yd.)
  for binding
Cotton fabric: floral print (¾ yd.)
Scissors

Notes

Gather a selection of beautiful threads for your embroidery. Threads such as pearl cotton, twisted silk, silk buttonhole twist, embroidery floss, some rayon threads commonly used for Brazilian embroidery, and silver and gold metal threads combine beautifully. Look through threads that have been left over from past projects. Do not discount anything.

Directions

1. Place muslin on wrong side of faille fabric, and baste together with sewing thread.

2. Place right side of dressmaker's carbon down on faille fabric.

3. Position enlarged Stitching Lines Diagram on top of dressmaker's carbon; tape down.

4. Using a tracing wheel or small blunt-ended instrument, trace all lines. Remove dressmaker's carbon.

5. Place marked fabric in a hoop and stitch, using Soft Case Stitch Diagram on pages 78–79 as pattern. Embroider all seam lines. Vary the threads and use a variety of different stitches (see pages 82–84 for Crazy Quilt stitches). On some lines, combine two or three stitches and different weights and colors of thread, including metal threads.

6. Check the completed work for loose threads or missed seam lines before proceeding.

7. Take a close look at the project, and tentatively decide areas that can use further embellishment. Consider the focal point.

8. Search in the button box, lace collection, and trinket drawer for charming items to sew on a special spot. If desired, stitch date on the piece.

9. Remove any bastings still in worked area.

10. If washable fabric and a blue washout marker have been used, markings should be removed before ribbons and other trims are added. To remove markings, soak entire embroidered piece in lukewarm water for 15 minutes or until all of the markings disappear completely.

11. Do not wring. Drip excess water, place on large towel, and pat smooth. Let fabric dry overnight, if necessary. Changing the towel a few times will speed up the process.

12. When embroidered piece is dry, it is ready for additional trim.

Finishing

Use ¼" seams.

1. Cut binding from ¼ yd. of lining fabric to measure 2¼" x 45". Set aside.

2. For pocket, fold inner pocket piece in half with right sides together to measure 8" x 6". Stitch across the 8" measurement to make a tube. Turn to the right side and press.

3. Place top (folded edge) on right side of pocket piece approximately 5½" from narrow end of lining. Pin securely to lining and sew both sides and bottom.

4. Place assembled lining on finished embroidery piece with wrong sides together. Baste around entire embroidery piece case to secure lining to case.

5. Bind narrow edge of case nearest to pocket. Bind entire case.

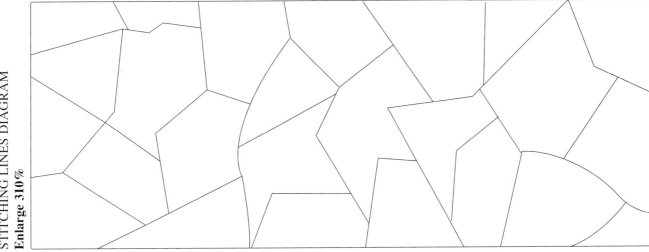

STITCHING LINES DIAGRAM
Enlarge 310%

SOFT CASE STITCH DIAGRAM   TOP   **Enlarge 115%**

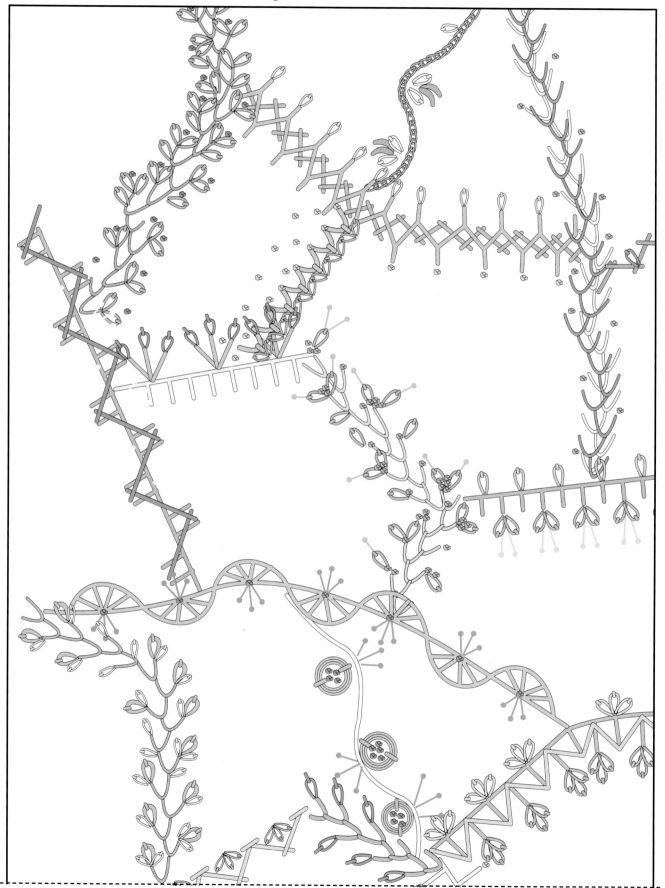

SOFT CASE STITCH DIAGRAM   BOTTOM   **Enlarge 115%**

𝒥ANET BENANDER began sewing at age 11. Throughout her life, she has tried and enjoyed all manner of fabric handcrafts, from making clothes and knitting to crewel embroidery and rug braiding.

In 1982, when she discovered quilting, all of these other pursuits took a backseat, and she became an enthusiastic and inquisitive quilter. She took classes and workshops, joined Narragansett Bay Quilters Guild, went to quilt shows and quilt shops, and quilted incessantly.

She took a part-time job at a quilt shop and taught a Beginner Sampler class, which led to teaching a variety of other classes. Her specialty, crazy-patch quilting, began in 1990 after being inspired by a Barbara Barber quilt. She found that the freedom from rules and precision was a pleasant change and enjoyed embellishing with all kinds of techniques and materials.

In 1992, with her husband, John, as a partner, she began a quilt show vending and mail order business. As a result of the exposure this has afforded, Janet says she has had the privilege of teaching many workshops for guilds and at shows, which include Mid-Atlantic Quilt Festival, East Coast Quilters Alliance Sampler, Vermont Quilt Festival, and Belle Grove Plantation.

Janet continues to enjoy quilting and association with other quilters through membership in Narragansett Bay Quilters Guild, Bayberry Quilters Guild, East Coast Quilters Alliance, and New England Quilters Guild.

PATCHES & POSIES

Materials

Muslin: 7" square (for piecing
    foundation)
Fabric scraps: various textures (5)
Dressmaker's carbon
Crewel needle #18
Embroidery hoop
Silk ribbon and rayon thread as
    outlined on Stitch Guide

Directions

1. Using Patchwork & Posies Stitch
Diagram on page 82 as pattern, piece
scraps of fabric together following
general instruction given for Victorian
Patchwork Vest, Step 3, Guidelines for
Piecing, on page 73.

2. Using dressmaker's carbon and
following manufacturer's instructions,
transfer stitch design from Patches &
Posies Transfer Diagram on page 82 to
fabric scrap used for center piece.

3. Stretch fabric taut on a hoop before
stitching.

4. Be sure to cover transfer lines on
fabric completely when stitching. Do
not clean until all stitching is completed, as transfer will be removed.

5. Refer to Stitch Guide for stitch and
color to be used (see Index for
stitches).

6. To end stitches, secure stitches in
place for each flower or small area
before beginning a new area. Tie a slip
knot on wrong side of needlework to
secure stitch in place and end ribbon.

Stitch Guide

Symbol	Stitch	Color	Size	Type
	Herringbone Stitch	Cream	18 ct.	Rayon Thread
	Straight Stitch	Green	18 ct.	Rayon Thread
	Couching Stitch	Lt. Green	18 ct.	Rayon Thread
	Straight Stitch	Olive Green	18 ct.	Rayon Thread
	Lazy Daisy Stitch	Olive Green	18 ct.	Rayon Thread
	Straight Stitch	Spruce Green	4 mm	Silk Ribbon
	Japanese Ribbon Stitch	Lt. Green	4 mm	Silk Ribbon
	Straight Stitch	Lt. Green	4 mm	Silk Ribbon
	Japanese Ribbon Stitch	Cream	4 mm	Silk Ribbon
	Spider Web Rose	Yellow	4 mm	Silk Ribbon
	Spider Web Rose	Rose	4 mm	Silk Ribbon
	Loop Petal Stitch	Yellow	4 mm	Silk Ribbon
	Straight Stitch	Rose	4 mm	Silk Ribbon
	Loop Petal Stitch	Lt. Blue	4 mm	Silk Ribbon
	Straight Stitch	Lt. Blue	4 mm	Silk Ribbon
	French Knot	Yellow	4 mm	Silk Ribbon
	Straight Stitch	Yellow	4 mm	Silk Ribbon
	French Knot	Lavender	4 mm	Silk Ribbon
	Fly Stitch with Straight Stitch	Lavender Lavender	4 mm 4 mm	Silk Ribbon Silk Ribbon
	Bullion Stitch	Gold	18 ct.	Rayon Thread
	Straight Stitch	Lt. Gold	18 ct.	Rayon Thread

PATCHES & POSIES STITCH DIAGRAM

ARROWHEAD STITCH

Come up at 1 on upper left; go down at 2. Come up at 3, and go down again at 2. Come up at 3, and go down at 4; continue to the end of the row.

CHEVRON STITCH

Bring needle up at 1, down at 2, up at 3, down at 4, up at 5, down at 6, back up at 7, down at 8, up at 9, and down at 10.

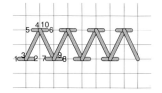

CROWS FEET STITCH

Bring needle up at 1, down at 2, up at 3, down at 4, up at 5, down at 6.

PATCHES & POSIES TRANSFER DIAGRAM

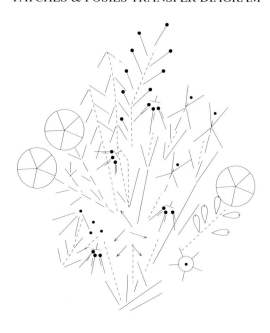

CRETAN STITCH

Working left to right, come up at 1 and go down at 2 and up at 3. Go down to the right at 4 and up at 5. Continue working in this manner until area is filled.

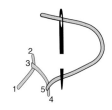

FAN STITCH

This stitch consists of Straight Stitches all radiating out from the same hole, forming a square shape. Stitches can skip a thread or be worked next to each other, depending on the coverage desired and thickness of thread used.

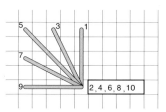

FEATHER STITCH

Come up at 1, go down at 2 and back up at 3, keeping the thread under the needle to hold it in a "V" shape. Pull flat. For second stitch, go down at 4 and back up at 5.

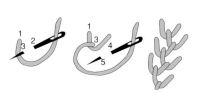

BUTTONHOLE STITCH VARIATIONS

(See page 58 for "Buttonhole Stitch.")

1. Half-Circle Buttonhole Stitch. Come up at 1 and down at 2, making a straight stitch. Come up at 1, down at 2 and up at 3; with needle tip over thread, pull needle through fabric at 3. Continue around from 1 at center to each of the spokes (4, 5, 6). To end, take needle to fabric back near 6.

2. Beads on long and short Buttonhole Stitch.

3. Elongated Half-Circle Buttonhole with bead at center.

4. Closed Buttonhole Stitch with beads.

5. Bead at center of motif (Half-Circle Buttonhole Stitch).

6. Three Straight Stitches, embellished with a single French Knot.

7. Alternate Lazy Daisy Stitch and three clusters of French Knots.

CHEVRON STITCH VARIATIONS

(See page 82 for "Chevron Stitch.")

1. Chevron Stitch with Lazy Daisy Stitch added to inside bottom.

2. Same as above, but the Lazy Daisy Stitch is almost equal in height to Chevron. Beads or French Knots could be added.

3. Chevron Stitch with single Lazy Daisy Stitch added to top. Complete all Chevrons before adding Lazy Daisy.

4. Elongated Chevron Stitch with Lazy Daisy Stitch added to top and then to inside.

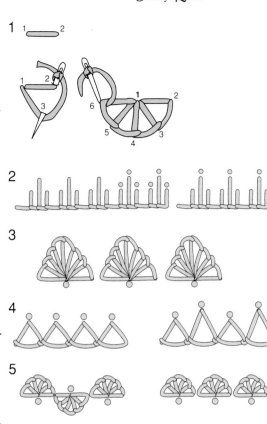

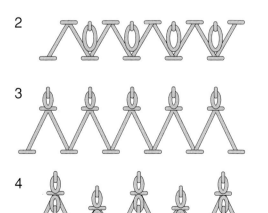

COMBINATION FOUNDATION STITCHES

(Two different stitches are integrated and completed simultaneously.)

1. Foundation stitch: alternating Herringbone Stitch and Chevron Stitch. Lazy Daisy Stitch added to Herringbone Stitch. Straight Stitch added to Chevron Stitch.

2. Foundation stitch: double alternating Chevron Stitch and Cretan Stitches (see page 82). Lazy Daisy Stitch added to Chevron Stitch. Cluster of three French Knots added to Cretan Stitch.

3. Foundation Stitch: Chevron Stitch and Herringbone Stitch. Herringbone tied with horizontal Straight Stitch. Vertical Straight Stitch added later. Beads added to both Chevron Stitch and Herringbone Stitch as indicated.

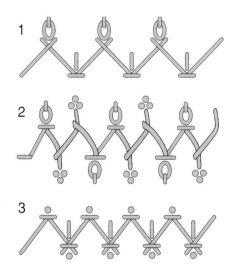

CRETAN STITCH VARIATION

(See page 82 for "Cretan Stitch.")
Complete Cretan Stitch first, then add Lazy Daisy Stitch between. Add bead or French Knot to bottom of Cretan Stitch.

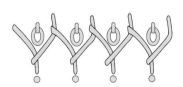

FEATHER STITCH VARIATION

(See page 82 for "Feather Stitch.")

1. Single alternating Feather Stitch with single French Knot.

2. Double alternating Feather Stitch with single French Knot.

3. Triple alternating Feather Stitch embellished with a seed bead on each outside "branch."

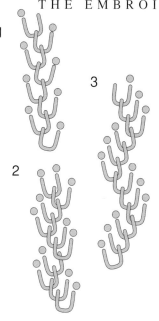

FLY STITCH VARIATION

(See page 71 for "Fly Stitch.")

1. Complete Fly Stitch with equal lengths. Add Lazy Daisy Stitch to "arms" of Fly Stitch. Stitch short Straight Stitches, alternating between the "Y" of stitch.

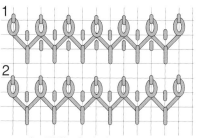

2. Work as before, except Straight Stitch is added to top only.

HERRINGBONE STITCH VARIATION

(See page 21 for "Herringbone Stitch.")

1. Regular or elongated Herringbone Stitch tied vertically with short Straight Stitch.

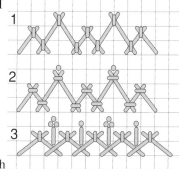

2. Elongated Herringbone Stitch tied horizontally with short Straight Stitch. Seed bead added to the longer stitch.

3. Long Straight Stitch and Herringbone Stitch embellished with alternating single and triple French Knots.

KNOTTED LAZY DAISY STITCH

Complete as Lazy Daisy Stitch, but tack with a French Knot. Bring the needle up, keeping thread flat, untwisted and full. Put the needle down through fabric and back up, but do not pull through.

Loosely wrap thread around needle tip one to three times. Holding finger over wrapped thread, insert needle down through fabric.

LAZY DAISY STITCH VARIATION

(See page 57 for "Lazy Daisy Stitch.")

1. Three Lazy Daisy Stitches with elongated centers. Stitched as a unit from left to right.

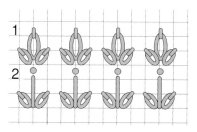

2. Lazy Daisy Stitch, long Straight Stitch, Lazy Daisy Stitch. Finish with seed bead.

LOOP PETAL STITCH

To make this stitch, come up through fabric at 1, form a small loop and go down at 2, piercing ribbon.

PISTIL STITCH

This stitch creates the look of a Straight Stitch with a French Knot on the end. Bring needle up through fabric at 1; smoothly wrap thread once (twice for a larger knot on end) around needle.

Hold thread securely off to one side and push needle down through fabric at 2, the length of the Straight Stitch portion of the stitch.

RUNNING STITCH

A line of Straight Stitches with an unstitched area between each stitch. Come up at 1 and go down at 2.

STRAIGHT STITCH VARIATION

(See page 37 for "Straight Stitch.")

1. Three Straight Stitches (good filler stitch).

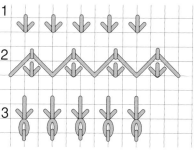

2. Make three Straight Stitches. Then complete inverted Fly Stitch with short tail.

3. Make three Straight Stitches. The center stitch is longer than the side stitches. Add Lazy Daisy Stitch to bottom.

CHERRY BLOSSOM FANS

JENNIFER ASHLEY TAYLOR has studied the precise Kurenai Kai Japanese embroidery technique for the past several years with Shay Pendray. In 1994, Jennifer became a teaching assistant to Shay for the first-, second-, and third-phase Japanese embroidery students at the Callaway School of Needle Arts. To broaden her exposure to the silk embroidery techniques practiced in Japan, Jennifer studied with Koyo Kida in 1993 and 1995.

Possessing a lifelong passion for learning, Jennifer has studied graphic art, interior design, and color at several colleges and universities. She received The Embroiderers' Guild of America Master Craftsman designation for Color in Embroidery in 1995. As a member of the National Academy of Needlearts Teacher Certification program, she teaches at schools, needlework guilds, and seminars nationwide.

Materials

Obi silk or medium-weight silk taffeta
   for ground fabric: 12" x 15"
Roller frame, 12" x 15", or small
   Japanese frame
Pearl cotton #12 for lacing
Milner's needles or Japanese needles
Japanese couching needles: #2 or #3
Couching thread: red and gold
Flat silk, 40 m tube: lt. peach (2–3),
   med. peach (1), dk. peach (1),
   med. green (1), yellow (1)
Japanese gold: #1 and #4
Laying tool
Pair of *koma* (see page 96)
Awl, if using a Japanese frame
45 degree triangle with mm markings
Wheat starch or tube of rice paste
Finishing paper

Stitch Guide

1   Body of Fan in Foreground: woven effect 4-to-1, #1 gold twist
2   Lattice Inlay on Fan in Foreground: lattice holding #1 gold
3   Outline of Fan in Foreground: *Kata-yori* couching *Kata-yori* twist
4   Cherry Blossom with Lattice: weft foundation layer
   Lattice: lattice holding #1 gold
5   Medium Cherry Blossom: weft foundation layer 2-to-1 twist
   Stamens: stamen effect with tadpole knots 1-to-2 S-twist
6   Light Cherry Blossom: weft foundation layer 2-to-1 twist
   Stamens: stamen effect with tadpole knots 1-to-2 S-twist
7   Dark Cherry Blossom: weft foundation layer 2-to-1 twist
   Stamens: stamen effect with tadpole knots 1-to-2 S-twist
8   Open Cherry Blossom: gold couching #4 gold
9   Leaves: horizontal foundation layer 2-to-1 twist
10   Main Strut on Fan in Distance: two pair nonstitchable #4 gold
11   Outline of Fan in Distance: one pair nonstitchable #4 gold
12 (a–d) Inner Struts on Fan in Distance: single thread nonstitchable #4 gold
13   Main Strut on Fan in Foreground: one pair nonstitchable #4 gold
14 (A–G) Inner Struts on Fan in Foreground: single thread nonstitchable #4 gold

Directions

1. Read all techniques and stitches on pages 94–102 before beginning.

2. Frame up ground fabric (see page 95 for "Framing Up").

3. Transfer the Cherry Blossom Fans Diagram on page 88 to ground fabric (see page 99 for "Transferring Japanese Design").

Section 1

Body of Fan in Foreground—woven effect. Make several hard twist 4-to-1 threads using lt. peach flat silk (see page 102 for "Woven Effect").

1. Begin at the top left section of the fan. Lay two threads parallel to the weft threads of the ground fabric, leaving a space the width of a third thread. Repeat over the whole area (see page 101 for "Weft Foundation Layer"). *Suggestion:* Put in temporary guidelines to help keep the stitches parallel to the weft threads of the fabric.

2. Half-hitch #1 gold to a large needle. Start stitching at the top left section of the fan, stitching the two threads of #1 gold perpendicular to the Step 1 stitches every 5 mm. Carefully lay the gold so that it is flat, and two #1 gold stitches are parallel.

3. About every 1 cm, couch over the two strands of gold. It isn't necessary to make the stitches at regular intervals. Couch the gold in the skipped areas beginning on left side.

4. Using a medium-hard 4-to-1 twist of lt. peach flat silk, fill in the weft foundation spaces.

5. With a 1-to-1 soft twist of the foundation color or the gold couching thread, secure the Step 4 weft foundation twist stitches with a loop stitch equal distance from the # 1 gold.

Section 2
Lattice Holding on Fan in Foreground. Using half-hitched #1 gold and a 45 degree triangle, establish stitches 1–2 and 3–4. (see "Lattice Holding" on page 96). Use the gold doubled, as in Step 2 of the "Woven Effect" on page 102 or a single strand for a lighter, softer look to the area. Complete all stitches in one direction, 5 mm apart, and then the other, using the "Laid Stitch" technique on page 96. Couch each intersection with gold couching thread or yellow 1-to-2 soft twist. Couching Stitch is 2–3 mm in length.

Section 3
Outline of Fan in Foreground—twist, *kata-yori* couching. Make a 36" to 40" length of lt. peach flat silk, twist *kata-yori*. Wind on a *koma*. Using a 1-to-2 lt. peach flat silk, soft twist, couch to the outside fan outline, every one or two twists of the *kata-yori*. Work in a clockwise direction (see page 94 for Couching Twisted Thread and page 99 for Twist, *Katayori*).

Section 4
1. Cherry Blossom with Lattice—weft foundation layer. Using lt. peach 2-to-1 flat silk thread, lay each stitch parallel to the weft threads of the fabric (see page 96 for "Laying Silk" and page 101 for "Weft Foundation Layer").

2. Lattice Holding. Using half-hitched #1 gold and a 45 degree triangle, establish stitches 1–2 and 3–4. (see page 96 for "Lattice Holding"). Use the gold doubled, as in Step 2 of the "Woven Effect" on page 102, or a single strand for a lighter, softer look to the area. Complete all stitches in one direction, 5 mm apart, and then the other, using the "Laid Stitch" technique. Couch each intersection with gold couching thread or yellow 1-to-2 soft twist. Couching Stitch is 2–3 mm in length (see page 94 for "Couching Japanese Gold").

Section 5
1. Medium Cherry Blossom—weft foundation layer. Using a med. peach 2-to-1 flat silk thread, lay each stitch parallel to the weft threads of the fabric (see page 96 for "Laying Silk" and page 101 for "Weft Foundation Layer").

2. Stamen Effect with Tadpole Knots— "S" twist. Yellow 1-to-2 soft "S" twist is used to make this variation of the single round knot. All the steps are identical, except the second stitch is placed away from the first stitch, giving the knot an extended tail (see page 98 for "Stamen Effect").

Section 6
1. Light Cherry Blossom—weft foundation layer. Using a lt. peach 2-to-1 flat silk thread, lay each stitch parallel to the weft threads of the fabric (see page 96 for "Laying Silk" and page 101 for "Weft Foundation Layer").

2. Stamen Effect with Tadpole Knots— "S" twist. Yellow 1-to-2 soft "S" twist is used to make this variation of the single round knot. All the steps are identical, except the second stitch is placed away from the first stitch, giving the knot an extended tail (see page 98 for "Stamen Effect").

Section 7
1. Dark Cherry Blossom—weft foundation layer. Using a dk. peach 2-

to-1 flat silk thread, lay each stitch parallel to the weft threads of the fabric (see page 96 for "Laying Silk" and page 101 for "Weft Foundation Layer").

2. Stamen Effect with Tadpole Knots— "S" twist. Yellow 1-to-2 soft "S" twist is used to make this variation of the single round knot. All the steps are identical, except the second stitch is placed away from the first stitch, giving the knot an extended tail (see page 98 for "Stamen Effect").

Section 8
Open Cherry Blossom—gold couching. Wrap #4 gold on each *koma*. Couch the flower outline with red or yellow couching thread or 1-to-2 soft twist yellow silk (see page 94 for "Couching Japanese Gold" and page 99 for "Twist, 1-to-2").

Section 9
Leaves—horizontal foundation layer. Using a med. green 2-to-1 flat silk thread, begin at the center of the leaf and work to the tip. Lay each stitch at a 45 degree angle to the main vein of each leaf. Pinhead and work from the center toward the flower. Leave one-point open space where the flower petals and leaves meet. If desired, add leaf main vein lines by couching #4 gold (see page 96 for "Horizontal Foundation Layer" and page 94 for "Couching Japanese Gold").

Section 10
Main Strut on Fan in Distance—two pair nonstitchable. Use #4 gold on a pair of *koma*. Sink all eight threads close to *kata-yori* twist outline of foreground fan (see page 98 for "Sinking Threads" and page 94 for "Couching Japanese Gold").

Sections 11 & 13
Outline of Fan in Distance and Main Strut on Fan in Foreground—one pair nonstitchable. Wind #4 gold on a pair of *koma*. Start outlining in center of strut. Use red couching thread to secure every other twist. Sink the threads at

both ends (see page 98 for "Sinking Threads" and page 94 for "Couching Japanese Gold").

Sections 12 a–d & 14 A–G
Inner Struts on Fan in Distance and Foreground—single thread non-stitchable. Use #4 gold on a *koma* and red couching thread to secure every other twist. Work the right side of each strut and then the left side. Sink the threads at both ends (see page 98 for "Sinking Threads" and page 94 for "Couching Japanese Gold").

Finishing
See page 94 for "Finishing, Japanese."

CHERRY BLOSSOM FANS DIAGRAM

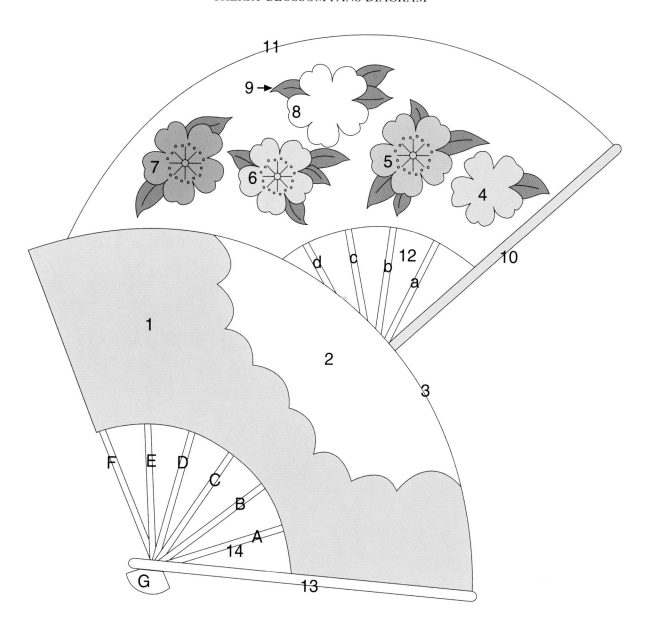

*K*AY STANIS is known internationally as a fiber artist, designer, and Certified Teacher of The Embroiderer's Guild of America (EGA) and Kurenai Kai Traditional Japanese Embroidery. She has passed levels I–III of the EGA Master Craftsman program in Silk and Metal. At the National Exhibits sponsored by EGA, her embroideries have received many Merit Award and Judges' Choice ribbons, including the 14th National Exhibit. One of these embroideries was on the cover of the June '95 issue of *Needle Arts*. She is juried into the advanced study group, Fiber Form, that has ongoing exhibits in galleries and museums throughout the United States.

Kay has studied in Paris at the L'Ecole de Broiderie D'Art (Lesage) and is fascinated with all types of embroidery, wishing to learn from the past to infuse the future with a mixture of tradition and new ideas.

Because of her work in traditional Japanese embroidery, Kay was invited to Japan to study with Master Saito at Kurenai Kai and was then certified and asked to teach in the United States. Her traditional Japanese embroidery has been shown on the cover of *Kurenai* magazine and by invitation in numerous exhibitions in the United States and Japan, including exhibits with the Smithsonian and with the Japanese Embassy in Washington, DC.

Kay maintains a studio in Wisconsin and teaches and lectures on silk and metal thread work on canvas and fabric in the United States and abroad for The American Needlepoint Guild (ANG), EGA, and independent groups. She has written three correspondence courses on silk and metal thread embroidery for EGA and is the chairperson of its Teacher Certification Committee. She has been or will be on the faculties of ANG national seminars, Callaway School of Needlearts, EGA national and regional seminars, and the National Academy of Needlearts. She also is a contributing designer to "The Embroidery Studio" on PBS.

CHERRY BLOSSOMS IN THE MIST

Materials

Silk fabric: 11" x 6" for ground fabric
Heavy cotton fabric, 11" x 4": white (2)
Flat silk: lt. pink, dk. red-violet,
    med. green
Outlining thread: white silk sewing
    thread
Couching silk: red silk sewing thread
Japanese gold #1
Needles: #6, #8, and #10 crewel, or
#10 sharp (quilting), or Japanese
    needle set (large handmade
    Japanese flat silk needle is
    suggested, if available); #22
    chenille for lacing
Stretcher bars (13" or 14" x 8")
Thumb tacks
Push pin
Lacing thread (1 yd.)
Saral tracing paper
Small book the depth of stretcher bars
    to fit inside 12" x 8" area
Dry ballpoint pen
Tekobari stroking needle
45 degree triangle with mm markings
Wheat starch or tube of rice paste
Finishing paper

Stitch Guide

1   Outline of the Fan: couched
    twisted silk and #1 gold
2   Mist: horizontal single layer with
    lattice holding
3   Realistic Cherry Blossoms:
    vertical single layer
    Stamens: random stamen effect
    Anthers: japanese knots
4   Buds: vertical single layer over
    self-padding
5   Leaves: diagonal single layer
    Veins: couched #1 gold
6   Stylized Cherry Blossoms:
    vertical single layer
    Stamens: straight stitches with
    sleeper stitch
    Centers: japanese knots

Directions

1. Read all techniques and stitches on
pages 94–102 before beginning.

2. Frame up ground fabric (see page 95
for Framing Alternative Diagram). Sew

a ½" hem to long sides of heavy cotton
fabric. With wrong sides together, sew
a ¼" seam along long sides of one piece
of heavy cotton fabric and silk fabric.
Repeat for other long side of silk fabric
with remaining piece of heavy cotton
fabric. At beginning and ending of
stitching line, oversew 1" to reinforce
edges. The right side will show the
seam, and seam edges will be on top as
fabric is framed up.

Assemble frame and mark center of
longer sides. Find the middle of fabric
by folding it in half and creasing the
very edge of heavy cotton fabric, on
top and bottom, with your fingers. Do
not crease the silk. Match center of
fabric to center line on frame bar and
tack. Tack approximately every 1–2" at
first, pulling out from center and
keeping grain lines of fabric straight.
As opposite side is tacked, keep the
fabric as taut as possible. There will be
more heavy cotton fabric than
necessary to meet the edge of frame.
This is available for holding as fabric is
pulled. Secure both sides, adjusting
tacks as necessary. Fill in space
between tacks so that they are spaced
½" to ¼" apart.

3. Transfer the Cherry Blossoms in the
Mist Diagram to ground fabric (see
page 99 for "Transferring Japanese
Design").

All section numbers correspond to
numbers on diagram.

Section 1

Outline of Fan. Using a #10 crewel
needle or small Japanese needle
threaded with silk sewing thread, work
Japanese Running Stitch (see page 98).

Section 2

1. Mist. Using a #6 crewel needle or
large, flat silk Japanese needle threaded
with two strands med. green flat silk,
work the weft foundation layer by
making Satin Stitches from top of the
design to the bottom. The stitch

direction is right to left (see page 96 for
"Laying Silk" and page 101 for "Weft
Foundation Layer"). Use the *tekobari*.

2. Using a #6 crewel needle or large
Japanese needle, thread with #1 gold
half-hitch. Work Lattice Holding (see
page 96).

3. Using a #10 crewel needle or small,
sharp Japanese needle threaded with
red silk sewing thread, couch lattice
(see page 96 for "Lattice Holding").

Section 3

1. Foreground Realistic Cherry
Blossoms. Using a #6 crewel needle or
large, flat silk Japanese needle threaded
with two strands lt. pink flat silk, work
vertical single layer by making Satin
Stitches toward you or right to left. Use
the *tekobari* (see page 96 for "Laying
Silk," page 101 for "Vertical Single
Layer," and page 97 for "Motif Shape
Rule").

2. Background Realistic Cherry
Blossoms. Using a #6 crewel needle or
large, flat, silk Japanese needle
threaded with one strand lt. pink flat
silk, work vertical single layer by
making Satin Stitches toward you or
right to left. Use the *tekobari*. Void the
area where petals come up against
foreground blossom.

3. Stamens of Realistic Cherry
Blossoms. Using #1 gold, work
Random Stamen Effect (see page 98).

4. Anthers of Realistic Cherry
Blossoms. Using #1 gold threaded in
half-hitch, work Japanese Knots,
scattering them across the cherry
blossoms (see page 96 for "Japanese
Knots").

Section 4

1. Buds. Using two strands dk. red-
violet flat silk, create padding for buds
(see page 98 for "Self-Padding").

2. Using a #6 crewel needle or large,

flat silk Japanese needle threaded with two strands dk. red-violet flat silk, work vertical single layer by making Satin Stitches toward you or right to left. Use the *tekobari* (see pages noted in Step 1, Section 3).

Section 5

1. Leaves. Using a #8 crewel needle or large Japanese needle threaded with med. green flat silk 2-to-1 twist, work diagonal single layer by making Satin Stitches toward you or right to left (see page 99 for "Twist 2-to-1," page 94 for "Diagonal Single Layer," and page 97 for "Motif Shape Rule").

2. Leaf Veins. Using #1 gold threaded in half-hitch, work leaf veins by making Straight Stitch. Couch with a sewing needle threaded with red silk sewing thread (see page 94 for "Couching Japanese Gold").

3. Bud Stems. Using #1 gold threaded in half-hitch, work stems of buds by making Straight Stitch. Couch with a

sewing needle threaded with red silk sewing thread (see page 94 for "Couching Japanese Gold").

Section 6

1. Stylized Cherry Blossoms. Using a #6 crewel needle or large, flat silk Japanese needle threaded with two strands lt. pink flat silk, work vertical single layer by making Satin Stitches toward you or right to left. Use the *tekobari* (see pages noted in Step 1, Section 3 on opposite page).

2. Stamens of Stylized Cherry Blossoms. Using #1 gold threaded in half-hitch, work Sleeper Stitch by making a short Straight Stitch that is parallel to top of petal and then working three Straight Stitches side by side perpendicular to and covering Sleeper Stitch completely (see page 98 for "Sleeper Stitch").

3. Center of Stylized Cherry Blossoms. Using a dk. violet-red flat silk 2-to-1 twist with #1 gold medium S-Twist,

work Japanese Knot in center of blossoms (see page 99 for "Twist, 2-to-1, with #1 Gold S" and page 96 for "Japanese Knot").

Section 7

Mist Outline. Using a med. green flat silk 2-to-1 medium twist, work outline by laying twist and couching in the valleys with a 1-to-2 twist med. green flat silk (see page 99 for "Twist 2-to-1" and page 94 for "Couching Twisted Thread").

Section 8

Fan Outline. Using a med. green flat silk 4-to-1 with two strands of #1 gold medium twist, work outline by laying twist and couching in the valleys with 1-to-2 twist med. green flat silk (see page 99 for "Twist, 4-to-1, with 2 Strands #1 Gold Z" and page 94 for "Couching Twisted Thread").

Finishing

See page 94 for "Finishing, Japanese."

CHERRY BLOSSOMS IN THE MIST DIAGRAM

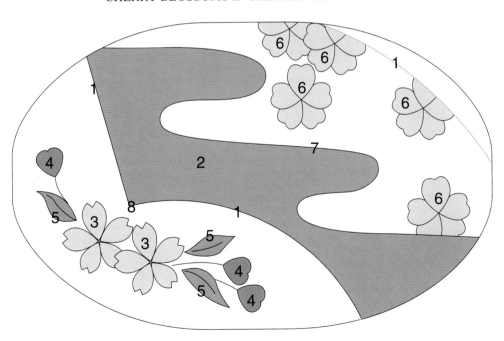

𝒥UDY SOULIOTIS is a teacher of canvas and fabric embroidery certified by the The Embroiderers' Guild of America in silk and metal thread work. She has studied with numerous instructors of Japanese embroidery. Judy lived in Japan for several years, and her knowledge of Asian customs and lifestyles along with her extensive training give her a unique insight into the intricacies of Japanese embroidery.

She has also studied in Japan for two-week sessions over four summers in Master Saito's intense class for advanced studies. Most recently, she was responsible for bringing an accomplished embroidery instructor from Kyoto to America to teach a group of eight advanced students. Recently, she displayed and demonstrated her embroidery in a two-woman show at the Morikami Museum in Florida, and had a one-woman show in Massachusetts.

An active student and teacher, Judy has taught nationally for The American Needlepoint Guild (ANG), The Embroiderers' Guild of America, The National Standards Council of America, The Greenbrier and Callaway Gardens, as well as for regional and local seminars. She is past president of the Massachusetts Chapter of ANG and was Northeast Area Representative for Chapter Development. She was also Director of the Steps to Perfection Program and now serves on the correspondence course committee for ANG.

BURDEN BUTTERFLY

Materials
Stretcher frame: 10" x 10"
Thumb tacks
Congress cloth: ecru (10" square)
Pencil with hard lead
Overdyed stranded silk: blue/red/gold shades (1 skein)
DMC fil or clair art: #282 gold (1 spool)
Tapestry needles: #22 and/or #24

Directions
1. Mount congress cloth on stretcher frame. Using a hard lead pencil, transfer the enlarged design to canvas.

2. Thread a #22 tapestry needle with one strand of gold doubled over about twice the stitching length. Begin Burden Stitch at the top right portion of right wing, placing the first stitch on the diagonal in the direction noted on Burden Butterfly Diagram. Find the least amount of counting to reach the end of the design area for the first stitch. After taking the stitch, make sure the double strands of gold lie next to each other. Bring needle up four horizontal or vertical threads apart (see page 94 for "Burden Stitch").

3. Thread a #22 tapestry needle with 3-ply of overdyed silk. Tack to secure the thread and make the first stitch. Complete Burden Stitch by working over the pair of gold with a pair of stitches that cover four intersections of the canvas (see page 94 for "Burden Stitch"). Skip two intersections and make another pair of stitches. Repeat to the end of the row.

4. Return to the gold again, and lay that thread on the diagonal, which should lie in the same diagonal row of holes as the silk stitches. Again, bring the gold to the top in the next hole to be stitched.

5. The second row of silk should fit between the stitches of the previous row. All stitches should come up a clean hole and, slanting the needle slightly, slip under the gold of the previous row.

6. When the right side, is finished, do the same on the left side except reverse the direction so that the wings will be mirror images.

7. The bottom sections of the wings are stitched in Basket-weave Stitch. Follow arrows on design chart for the stitching direction (see Basket-weave Stitch).

8. The inner top wings are stitched with one strand of gold in a horizontal Satin Stitch (see page 22 for "Satin Stitch").

9. The body of the butterfly is stitched with a double strand of gold. Pad the body first with a few horizontal stitches in each section. (This will raise up the body to give it some shape.) Then use a vertical Satin Stitch on each body section (see page 22 for "Satin Stitch"). Note the curve of the stitches at the head of the butterfly.

10. Work the antennae and all outlining with one strand of gold. Use the Outline Stitch for the antennae and the top edge of the upper wings (see page 58 for "Outline Stitch"). Use the Chain Stitch for the bottom edge of the upper wings and the inner wing outline (see page 57 for "Chain Stitch"). Finish as desired.

BASKET-WEAVE STITCH
Work the area by stitching rows diagonally in the direction of the arrows on project diagram. Come up at 1 and go down at 2. Come up at 3, go down at 4.

Continue building on the diagonal, always going down (not coming up) in a previously filled hole, until area is complete.

The backside of stitching will have basketweave appearance.

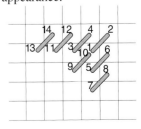

BURDEN
BUTTERFLY
DIAGRAM
**Enlarge
142%**

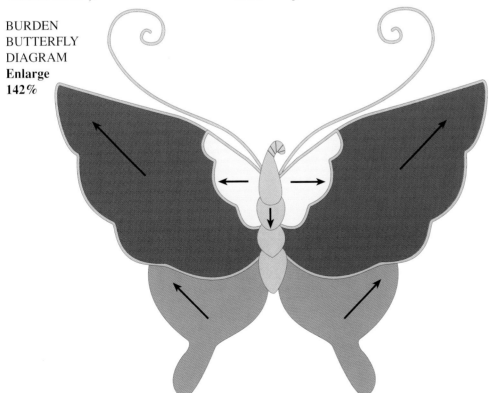

BEGINNING & ENDING THREAD WITH PINHEAD STITCH

Make a small knot in the end of the silk or gold; come up through the underside of the fabric; go back down through the fabric very close to the first stitch, making a tiny (less then ⅛") Pinhead Stitch. The knot remains on the underside at all times (see page 101 for Warp & Weft Threads Diagram). To end, gently come up between the rows of metal or under previous stitches, being careful not to catch the other threads, and make two small pinheads. Then bring the thread up through stitch area a third time and clip closely. In Japanese embroidery, the frame is usually not turned over for any reason (see page 101 for Warp & Weft Threads Diagram).

BURDEN STITCH DIAGRAM

Place the first stitch on the diagonal. Bring needle up four horizontal or vertical threads apart. Thread second needle. Work over the diagonal stitch with a pair of stitches that cover four intersections of the canvas. Skip two intersections and make another pair of stitches. Repeat to end of the row.

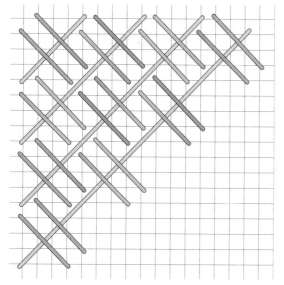

COUCHING JAPANESE

To start, pinhead and then couch over the first thread. Stitches should be perpendicular to the gold and spaced every other twist of the metal.

If using two gold threads, pinhead again. Add the second gold thread and stitch directly over both threads. When stitching a sharp corner, separate the pair of gold threads and stitch the outer thread once by itself at the corner to make a sharp turn.

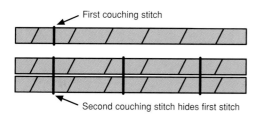

First couching stitch

Second couching stitch hides first stitch

COUCHING, TWISTED

Couch laid twisted thread, such as Twist, *Kata-yori*. Twist the pair of laid threads so that they form elongated "S" shapes every 3 mm, and couch in the valleys where the two strands cross one another.

COUCHING THREAD OR SILK SEWING THREAD

Silk sewing thread is used for couching and Japanese Running Stitch. Threads used for couching should be anchored with a Pinhead Stitch in an area not far from the beginning of the couching that will be covered by the embroidery.

DIAGONAL SINGLE LAYER

Diagonal stitches are always worked to follow the angle created by the Z-twist. If twists are turned on their sides, a sharp angle is created from the upper right to the lower left. The leaf axis runs from point to point down the center of the leaf. Stitch the twist at the shape's angle. See page 97 for "Motif Shape Rule, Cherry Blossom," and page 99 for "Stitching Direction" and "Stitching Sequence." The first stitch can be made slightly away from the tip to establish a good diagonal. Go back and fill in the area after a few stitches.

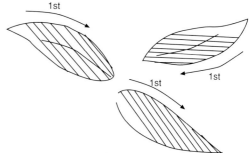

FINISHING, JAPANESE

1. Right side of embroidery: Check for missing stitches.

2. Underside of embroidery: Cut all ends to 3 mm or less.

3. Underside: Put a small amount of rice or wheat paste in the palm of your hand. Work around to form a thin film about the consistency of heavy cream. Apply to the embroidered areas with your fingertips. Work in the direction of the stitches, being very careful to stay on the embroidery to avoid paste showing through to the right side.

4. Underside: Dampen a small towel thoroughly. Wring out completely. Gently wipe the back side of the fabric, embroidered areas first.

5. Right Side: Dip a towel in water and wring it out slightly. Fold towel in half. Lay it over the plate of a dry, very hot iron. Hold it to the underside of embroidery about 1" from the glued areas. Do not allow it to touch the fabric. Let the steam come through the embroidered areas first; then move the iron parallel to the weft threads under the whole piece. Remove the towel, and let the iron cool to the lowest setting.

6. Right Side: Lay the smooth (shiny) side of finishing paper over the embroidery. With a very cool, dry iron, move it over the embroidery parallel to the weft threads. The iron should barely touch the finishing paper so that no weight is on the fabric. Keep the other hand on the underside directly under the iron to check the temperature and support the embroidery and fabric. The purpose is to enhance the brightness of the silk.

7. Underside: Lay finishing paper over the entire area. Iron it lightly in the weft direction to dry the fabric.

8. Repeat Steps 3 through 7 two more times.

9. Let the fabric dry thoroughly before removing it from the frame.

10. Unframe in the reverse order you framed up.

FRAMING ALTERNATIVE DIAGRAM

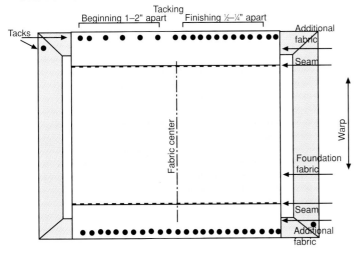

FRAMING UP

Mount fabric so that pattern is centered in opening. Attach top and bottom edges to roller bars. Tighten so that fabric is as taut as possible. Then lace selvage sides with #8 or #12 pearl cotton. First turn frame on its side so that short side is toward you. To lace, put thread in needle, but do not cut from spool until side is laced. Hold frame so that side to be laced is horizontal and closest to you. Working from right to left, come up from the underside of fabric approximately 1" away from frame's now "vertical" bar or roller bar (side with tacks along edge) and ¼"–⅛" from edge of fabric, stitching in selvage or hem. Take needle down through fabric, making a stitch about ½"–¾" long. After passing through fabric, bring up needle between fabric and frame, not catching fabric, and wrap thread around outside of frame. Again bring needle up through the fabric about ½"–¾" from previous stitch. Continue making lacing stitches until reaching approximately 1" from

the opposite side of the frame. Cut thread at other end off spool and tie to frame securely. Turning frame around, repeat on other side.

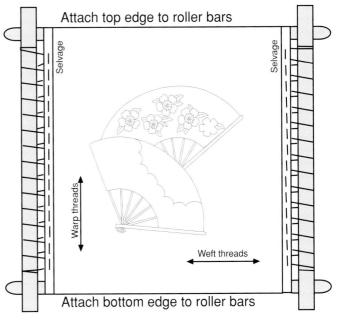

Attach top edge to roller bars

Selvage — Selvage

Warp threads

Weft threads

Attach bottom edge to roller bars

FRAMING UP, TIGHTENING LACING

Again working from right to left, insert a small, rounded stick, unsharpened pencil, or awl under thread where it is carried across edge of frame and pull diagonally and horizontally to tighten each stitch. Work all the way across. Pull gently, but firmly, and not vertically. If pulled vertically, the fabric can rip and/or the thread can break. In this first tightening, the idea is to make the backing fabric firm in frame, but not drum tight. At the far left side of frame, push a tack partly into the wood. When you have finished tightening, wrap thread end around this tack to help keep the tension. Add a few overhand knots on tack and push it in all the way. This should hold your lacing string taut. When you need to tighten again, just pull the tack out and repeat the procedure above. Do both sides. Fabric surface should be tight enough to bounce a coin. Check tension of fabric each time before stitching. Use a device such as a clamp that will hold frame steady and flat while working embroidery.

HALF-HITCH

Cut a strand of #1 gold (stitchable) twice the length needed for stitching. Lightly fold in half and place loop through eye of needle. Insert the ends through loop and pull until knot is snug against eye.

HORIZONTAL FOUNDATION LAYER

Laying threads at a 90 degree angle to main vein of each leaf (see page 101 for Warp & Weft Threads Diagram).

JAPANESE GOLD #1

Japanese gold can be sewn in and out of foundation in same manner as any embroidery thread (stitchable). It is necessary to thread #1 gold onto needle so that it will not become twisted during stitching and strands stay parallel. The usual manner is to attach thread in a double strand with a half-hitch through eye of needle (see page 95 for Half-hitch).

JAPANESE GOLD, ONE PAIR NONSTITCHABLE

Two gold strands couched as one with red couching thread (see page 94 for "Couching Japanese Gold").

JAPANESE GOLD, SINGLE THREAD NON-STITCHABLE

One gold strand couched with red couching thread (see page 94 for "Couching Japanese Gold").

JAPANESE GOLD, TWO PAIR NONSTITCHABLE

Stitch the first pair on the design outline, and add the second pair next to it.

JAPANESE KNOT

Using an S-twisted thread (see page 100), bring needle up through fabric and throw thread so that a loop forms to the left of hole where the thread is emerging from fabric. "Step" over loop and pierce fabric next to, but not in, same hole. As needle disappears below fabric and two loops are left on top, put two or three fingers through the second loop and spread it so that first loop is pulled tight against hole. Now pull needle and thread all the way down. A knot will form against the hole in fabric.

KOMA

Specially designed spools to help maintain wrap and twist of the thread.

KOMA, WRAPPING

Tie #4 gold on the *koma*. Holding a length of gold in the left hand and the *koma* in the right hand, twist the gold on the *koma* toward your body with a beckoning motion, keeping a firm tension. When the gold tightens on the thread core, wrap away from your body for a few twists. Then return to wrapping toward your body.

LAID STITCH

Conserves thread—but it is harder to lay threads smooth (Compare to Satin Stitch, Japanese).

LATTICE HOLDING

To keep flat silk stitches from moving, work holding stitches over top of area. Using a 45 degree triangle, establish direction with stitches 1–2 and 3–4. Complete all stitches in one direction and then the other. Beginning at extreme upper left of motif, couch each intersection, working in rows from top to bottom, with red or gold couching thread or yellow 1-to-2 soft twist. These stitches are normally made parallel to the Satin Stitches but can also be made perpendicular.

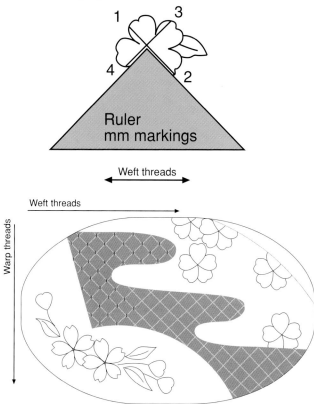

LAYING SILK

The result of this technique is that silk lays flat against fabric and shines. If shine is missing, silk is not tight enough. After the Pinhead, the needle is brought up at the beginning point with the left hand. The right hand pulls the needle through the fabric. Under the fabric, the middle finger of the left hand catches the loop of the silk to keep it taut. As the thread extends to the full length, give a little tug to set the stitch.

The right hand puts the needle down through the top of the fabric. The left hand takes hold of the needle and pulls silk down to the back of fabric until there is a 4–5 cm loop remaining on the surface. Then, with the right hand, pick up the laying tool and stroke the loop two or three times only in the direction of the stitch—never back and forth—to get all the filaments or sugas spreading and laying parallel to each other. With the left hand, pull the thread taut (see diagram on top of opposite page).

When thread is on underside of frame, try to keep tension on the thread. Place stroking needle where thread enters fabric until needle can be poked up to start next stitch. Now let go of needle and, with the left hand, run your fingers along silk until reaching loop. Take hold of the loop with left hand and, with right hand, pull needle up so that tension is kept on thread. As you draw the needle and thread through fabric, allow left hand to follow the loop up. Both hands will be moving, keeping tension even.

When all thread is on top, place tip of first finger of the left hand on underside of fabric where thread is emerging. Keep your fingertip on silk, until next stitch is placed and needle is again in fabric.

Move left hand on underside of frame to needle and start drawing thread down. Stroke thread with right hand when loop is left on the surface. Now draw thread down, keeping the tension. Repeat the process.

Flat silk requires keeping stitches far apart so that silk can spread and stay parallel. Stitches should be five to six per 5 mm space depending on the thickness of silk.

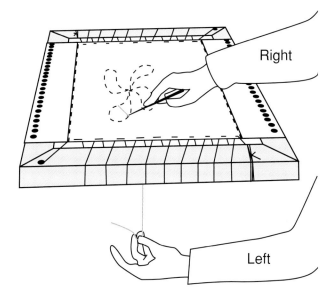

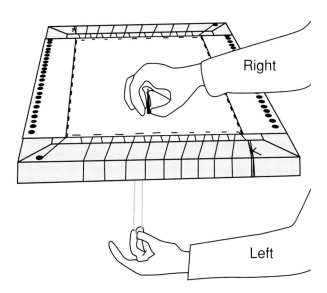

LAYING TOOL
Metal, wood, or plastic tool used to assist laying the sugas of silk flat against the ground fabric.

LOOP STITCH, OR TACK HOLDING
Come up from the underside of the fabric to the top, encircle the thread, and go down through the fabric very close to first stitch.

MOTIF SHAPE RULE, CHERRY BLOSSOM
These are stitches so that the outer- and innermost points are exaggerated. The stitch should extend one pin point beyond the outer point and should retreat one pin point inside inner points.

NONSTITCHABLE THREAD
Japanese gold, *Kata-yori* twist, or other thread that cannot be threaded through a needle or stitched through fabric.

ONE-POINT OPEN SPACE
Approximately the width of the needle (see page 101 for Warp & Weft Threads Diagram).

PINHEAD
A tiny stitch to anchor a thread inside the design area.

PROTECTING IN-PROGRESS WORK
Always keep foundation covered when you are not working. Tissue paper or plastic wrap should be placed next to foundation fabric. While you are working, keep other areas covered so that they don't become damaged by process of working. When not working on embroidery, keep it covered with tissue paper or plastic wrap and a heavier weight of fabric. A square of any fabric will work, and many people like to use scarves.

RANDOM STAMEN EFFECT

This technique is used to give a naturalistic effect. Imagine a circle suspended over the cherry blossom, and stitch Straight Stitches of random length dividing up the circle. The first stitch always comes from the middle of the "face" petal. After you have made eight stitches, bring needle up at base of face petal where stitches cross and make a Cross-Stitch that drags all the stamen down to this new center.

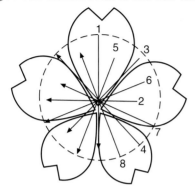

RUNNING STITCH, JAPANESE

Used to outline all man-made projects in Japanese embroidery. It is also used to mark outlines of embroidery area if motifs run off edge. Using silk sewing thread, white or the color of

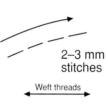

2–3 mm stitches

Weft threads

fabric, outline the shape and edge of design outline where shape touches it. This stitch is made up of 2–3 mm stitches with a very small space between each stitch. The length of the stitch varies as it moves around a curve; the maximum length is approximately 10 mm. The stitches should be kept slightly outside the design line.

SATIN STITCH, JAPANESE

Threads lie next to each other for a filled-area effect.

1 3 5

2 4 6

SELF-PADDING

To make buds appear to be bursting with life, self-padding is added under final stitching. Self-padding means to stitch with same

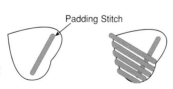

Padding Stitch

fiber that final layer is stitched. Only one stitch is made in opposite direction of final layer.

SELVAGE

Tightly woven finished edges of fabric.

SINGLE ROUND KNOT

See "Stamen Effect" in next column.

SINKING NEEDLES

Secure a large needle to fabric so that it will not move. Using one strand of silk, make a hard Z-twist by threading

the silk through the eye before dividing the thread to begin the undertwist. Complete twisting. Put wheat paste on end to maintain twist. Run the end of the thread back through the needle eye to create a loop (see Sinking Threads Diagram).

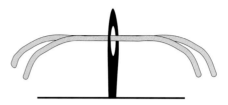

SINKING THREADS DIAGRAM

Cut couched thread to 2–3 mm of line end. Plunge sinking needle through fabric catching midpoint of the nonstitchable thread with loop. Quickly pull loop through fabric.

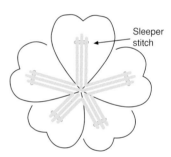

2–3 mm

Couching threads

Fabric

SLEEPER STITCH

On the cherry blossoms, place a stitch perpendicular to the foundation stitch so that other stitches that will be placed on top will not sink into foundation stitches.

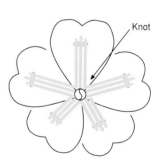

Sleeper stitch

STAMEN EFFECT

Using an S-twist thread, make a sideways "e" (see "Japanese Knot" on page 96). Pass the needle through the loop and down into the fabric, just to the left of the first hole.

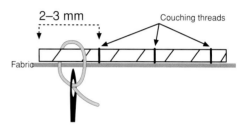

Knot

Pull the needle through the fabric. As you do so, a second loop is formed. Put two fingers of the right hand through the loop to spread it out and close the circle at the surface of the fabric. To control the size of the knot, insert the laying tool into the loop as you spread the loop. The knot forms as the thread goes to the underside of the fabric.

STATIONARY OBJECT

Keep threads from moving while twisting by securing them to a stationary object, such as a push pin. Gather strands in right hand with thumb underneath them. Keeping them taut, turn hand over and insert thumb in resulting loop. Wrap loop around object, and pull tight to secure threads. Divide strands in half, positioning half to left of object and half to right of object in preparation for twisting.

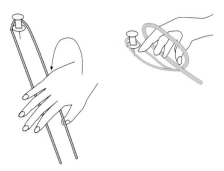

STITCHING DIRECTION
Right to left, top to bottom, and clockwise. To execute stitches, the right hand always works stitches on top and the left hand always remains on underside of embroidery. Begin at top left of each motif, and stitch to bottom right.

STITCHING SEQUENCE
Traditional Japanese embroidery is based on the stitcher recognizing a foreground area from the background. The embroidery is worked from foreground to background with voided spaces or one-point open spaces left where the motifs overlap. The foreground to background areas are marked numerically and should be stitched in that order.

STRAND, OR SUGA
Composed of 12 sugas that are often divided for twisting and laying flat foundations.

TRANSFERRING JAPANESE DESIGN
Remember to leave one-point open space around all leaves where they intersect with petals so that Running Stitch or transfer marks do not show. When entire design is transferred, check and make sure you are happy with it before removing pins. It is difficult to line everything up in the exact same way again if you forgot an area. Use one of the following methods:

1. Using tissue paper with a shiny side, draw design on dull side. Place shiny side down over the middle of the fabric. Using a Running Stitch and 1-to-2 soft twist, stitch each outline on the design line with the color of the area.
OR

2. Using a light box and a permanent thin-line pen, lightly transfer design outline. Practice first.
OR

3. Place design paper on foundation in desired area, and pin on one edge in two places. Place transfer paper (either dressmaker's carbon or Saral) between design paper and foundation with marking side down. Place a book the size of design area and at least the thickness of frame under design area for support.

Using a ballpoint pen with no ink left, trace design onto fabric, starting from center and working out to edges. After you have made a few marks, lift paper without removing pins and check to see how well it is transferring. You may have to adjust the pressure on pen.

TWIST
There are two types of twist— the S-Twist and the Z-Twist. To make twisted thread, use a stationary object to loop threads over. This can be an awl, a screw in a frame holder, a needle inserted in the foundation, a push pin, or even a doorknob. Just be sure that it is stable and won't move around as tension is put on it, that it is not too large in diameter, and that threads will still loop over it while it is firmly held in place.

Allow thread to un-spool between your fingers from underneath, holding the tube in your hand. Do not be tempted to let it curl off the end of tube, as this will add twist onto the strand. There is also a chance that silk filaments will snag on cardboard of tube.

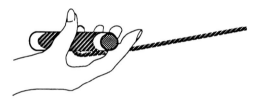

TWIST, Z, 1-TO-2 SOFT
Makes two thin twists from one strand of flat silk. Divide a strand in half. Set aside six sugas. Divide six sugas in half. Using three sugas, make a soft undertwist. Hold in teeth, while undertwisting the second set of three sugas. Put both together and overtwist. Repeat for remaining six sugas.

TWIST, Z, 2-TO-1
Makes one twist from two strands of flat silk.

TWIST, S, 2-TO-1, WITH #1 GOLD
Makes one twist from two strands of flat silk combined with one strand of gold.

TWIST, Z, 4-TO-1
Makes one twist from four strands of silk.

TWIST, Z, 4-TO-1, WITH 2 STRANDS #1 GOLD
In this case, you will need to add #1 Gold to both sides of the stationary object before twisting thread. Remember to add the extra undertwist before combining with gold.

TWIST, Z, *KATA-YORI* 5½ + ½
Undertwist (right hand) 5½ strands as hard as possible

without kinking the silk. Add ½ strand. Leave slack in the strand. Overtwist (left hand), until a satisfactory twist is achieved. Holding tightly, wrap *Kata-yori* around a pair of chop sticks or round tube. Wet the thread with water, allow to dry completely, and wrap on *koma*.

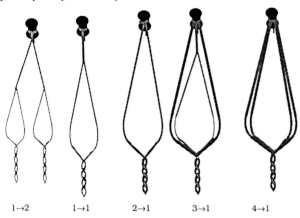

| 1→2 | 1→1 | 2→1 | 3→1 | 4→1 |

TWIST, OVERTWIST

The second palm of the hand you use to twist the strands of flat silk to complete a twisted thread (see "Twist, Z-Twist," Steps M–O).

TWIST, S-TWIST

Follow Steps A through F for "Twist, Z-Twist." The undertwist Steps G through J are done using the left palm. Complete Steps K and L. The overtwist Steps M, N and O are done with the right palm. Complete Step P.

TWIST, HARD, MEDIUM & SOFT

Use varied tension when twisting strands for differnt tensions.

TWIST, UNDERTWIST

The first palm of the hand you use to twist the strands of flat silk to make a twisted thread, i.e., the right hand for a Z-twist (see "Twist, Z-Twist" Steps G–J) and the left hand for an "S" twist.

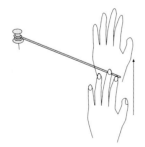

TWIST, Z-TWIST

Use stationary object to twist silk.

A. With a tube of flat silk in the palm of the right hand, pull off 36" to 48" with the left hand. Slip the silk around stationary object.

B. With the tube of silk still in your right hand, continue to reel off a length equal to the amount in the left hand. Cut off and set silk tube aside.

C. Steps A and B are the beginning steps for a 2-to-1 twist.

D. For a 3-to-1 twist, repeat Step A; for a 4-to-1 twist, repeat Steps A and B; for a *Kata-yori* twist, repeat Steps A and B twice.

E. Hold the equal lengths in the left hand. Extend the left hand so that the silk is slightly taut. With the right hand, make a loop and put it over the stationary object to anchor the thread.

F. Divide the strands of silk equally and spread to the right ("R") and left of the anchored thread.

G. Put the "R" strands in the base of the palm of the right hand. Hold in place with the fingertips of the left hand.

H. Run the left-hand fingertips up the palm of the right hand to the fingertips, twisting the "R" silk as it moves along the path. Keep the thread under tension.

I. Pick up the partially twisted thread and repeat Steps G and H, until you have the desired twist, usually three or four times.

J. Hold the twisted thread in your teeth to maintain the tension and the twist. Repeat Steps G, H, and I for the "L" strands.

K. Next, test the uniformity of the undertwists by holding the ends of "R" and "L" in one hand. Grasp both twists about 6"–10" from the other hand. Move hands toward each other. If the loops are equal, go to the next step. Otherwise, loosen or overtwist to get both twists even.

L. Tie the undertwists together with a single overhand knot, making sure both are equal length.

M. Now overtwist by putting the tied twists in the base of the palm of the left hand. Hold in place with the fingertips of the right hand.

N. Run the right-hand fingertips up the palm of the left hand to the fingertips, twisting the silk as it moves along the path. Keep the silk under tension.

O. Pick up the partially twisted thread and repeat Step N until you have the desired overtwist, usually one less twist than the number of undertwists.

P. Remove the twist from the stationary object and knot this end. Cut off half-knot made in Step L and thread the opposite end of the twist into the needle.

VERTICAL SINGLE LAYER

Stitches worked vertical to the motif. The stitches progress from center to outside of shape in cherry blossoms. Cherry blossoms have a distinct shape in Japanese embroidery. They will always appear with a dip—either a notch or heart-shaped dip—in the center of the motif. When they have a notch, they are considered more realistic than when they have rounded-off petals. Cherry blossoms also have a distinct order of stitching. Start with the "face" petal (the largest one); then stitch the two "hand" petals (medium size); then the "feet" petals (smallest). Always use the Motif Shape Rule (see page 97). First, stitch in the center. Stitches then progress to the right. After first half is done, stitches again start next to the center stitch and work left.

The stylized cherry blossoms will have a voided area or one-point open space next to the petal that has already been stitched.

WARP & WEFT THREADS DIAGRAM

Direction the fabric threads are woven.

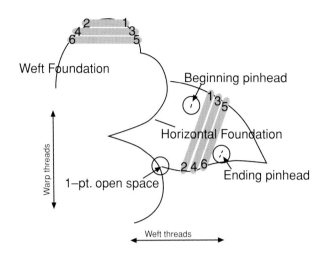

WEFT FOUNDATION LAYER

Laying threads parallel to the weft fabric threads. Work Satin Stitches from the top left of the motif to the bottom right. The needle comes up on the right and goes down on the left. The first stitch should be slightly down from the edge to establish a long line for the eye to follow, up at 1 and down at 2. Begin again at 3. After several stitches, go back and put in stitches near edge. This is the only time you should work from the previous stitches up. Using the flat silk, follow directions for Laying Silk on page 96. Fill entire area, keeping stitches inside outline running stitches (see Warp & Weft Threads Diagram above).

Realistic Cherry Blossom

Stylized Cherry Blossom

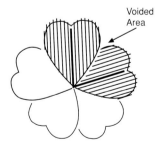

Voided Area

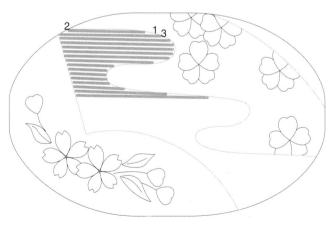

WOVEN EFFECT

1. Lay two 4-to-1 hard twist threads parallel to the weft threads, leaving space for one thread; repeat until fan area is covered.

2. Half-hitch #1 gold and lay perpendicular to the foundation stitches laid in Step 1; use Satin Stitch method to lay gold at 5 mm intervals.

3. About every 1 cm, couch the #1 gold in the open spaces between the weft pairs using gold couching thread. It isn't necessary to have stitches at regular intervals.

4. Using a medium-hard 4-to-1 twist, fill in the weft foundation spaces.

5. With a 1-to-1 soft twist of the foundation color or the gold couching thread, work a Loop Stitch over the Step 4 weft foundation twist stitches.

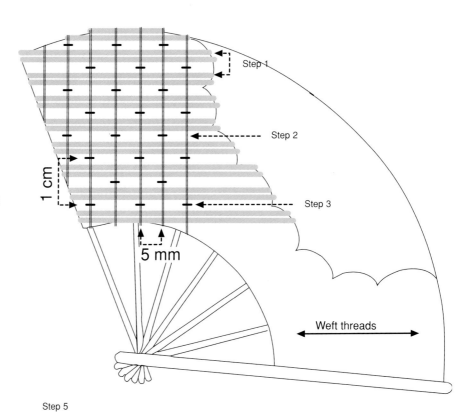

WRAPPING A STATIONARY OBJECT

Unspool desired length of thread, 24"–36" (see page 99 for "Twist"). Wrap around stationary object from 1 to 2. Unspool another equal length of thread. Wrap around stationary object from 3 to 4. Thread is now ready for Stationary Object (see page 98).

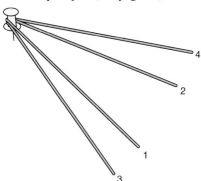

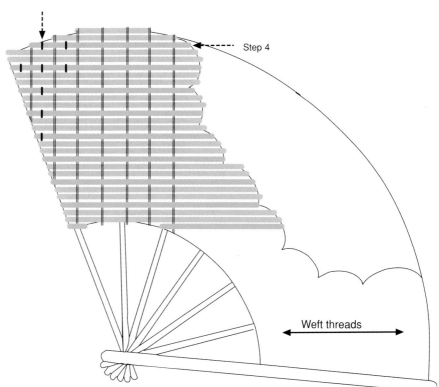

"ENDER TWISTED STRANDS plied of flax and silk, Stitch hearts that never grieve—blooms that never wilt."

These gentle words found on a softly faded sampler beckon one to the quiet world of Shepherd's Bush, a needlework haven located in Ogden, Utah, nestled between the shores of the Great Salt Lake and the beautiful snow-capped Wasatch range of the Rocky Mountains.

In 1984, Teri Richards (left) and her sister Tina Richards Herman (right) opened the retail shop which is said to evoke a nostalgia of the gentle, lifelong pursuit of fine handwork.

With a thriving retail business and Tina's new baby in tow, the two women then launched their design business in 1987 under the name, Shepherd's Bush Printworks.

Since opening their shop, Teri has taught countless basket-weaving and needlework classes. Her work in the shop has given her the opportunity to do a variety of different things, from sales, teaching, and designing to dyeing hundreds of yards of fabric to be used in the kits they produce. Teri began publishing her own work in 1990. She enjoys designing with the larger weaves of fabrics, such as 18 linen and Klostern. She loves to see how the colors blend and come alive.

Through the shop, Teri and Tina have taught thousands of children in their weekly children's classes. "We like to start them on something big to make learning fun and exciting. Projects like this are great for beginning stitchers," says Teri.

Children's Projects

FAMILIES ARE FOREVER

The "Families are Forever" design was stitched on ivory Herta 6, and the finished design size is 6⅛" x 8⅝". The fabric was cut 13" x 15". See Index for stitches.

Fabric	Design Size
Aida 11	3⅜" x 4¾"
Aida 14	2⅝" x 3¾"
Aida 18	2" x 2⅞"
Hardanger 22	1⅝" x 2⅜"

Anchor   DMC Pearl Cotton #3

Step 1: Cross-Stitch (1 strand)

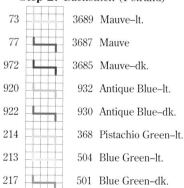

300		745	Yellow–lt. pale
73		3689	Mauve–lt.
77		3687	Mauve
972		3685	Mauve
130		799	Delft–med.
920		932	Antique Blue–lt.
922		930	Antique Blue–dk.
214		368	Pistachio Green–lt.
213		504	Blue Green–lt.
217		501	Blue Green–dk.

Step 2: Backstitch (1 strand)

73		3689	Mauve–lt.
77		3687	Mauve
972		3685	Mauve–dk.
920		932	Antique Blue–lt.
922		930	Antique Blue–dk.
214		368	Pistachio Green–lt.
213		504	Blue Green–lt.
217		501	Blue Green–dk.

FAMILIES ARE FOREVER   Stitch Count: 37 x 52
Each grid square = 1 stitch

LOVE

The "Love" design was stitched on white Herta 6, and the finished design size is 2½" x 2⅞". The fabric was cut 9" x 9". See Index for stitches.

Fabric	Design Size
Aida 11	1⅜" x 4¾"
Aida 14	1⅛" x 1¼"
Aida 18	⅞" x 1"
Hardanger 22	⅝" x ¾"

LOVE   Stitch Count: 15 x 17
Each grid square = 1 stitch

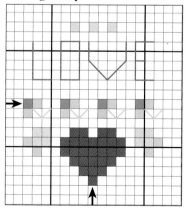

*A*NN BENSON is a well-known designer and author. To date, she has written four books—*Beadweaving, Beadwear, Beadwork Basics* and *Two-hour Beaded Projects* for Sterling Publishing Co., Inc. Her work for international corporations includes designing toys, board games, and children's craft kits.

Ann has said that, for her, indulging in the creative process is a mental oasis. She compares her work to a vitamin—needing it every day and not feeling quite right with-out it.

She uses various techniques and materials in her beaded designs. She incorporates fine threads and antique, handmade, and manufactured beads of all sorts and sizes on textile sur-faces and loomed and woven pieces.

In her leisure time, Ann enjoys bicycling and cross-country skiing, and she is currently working on a second novel.

Ann and her family reside in Amherst, Massachusetts.

LOOMED HEADBAND & EARRINGS

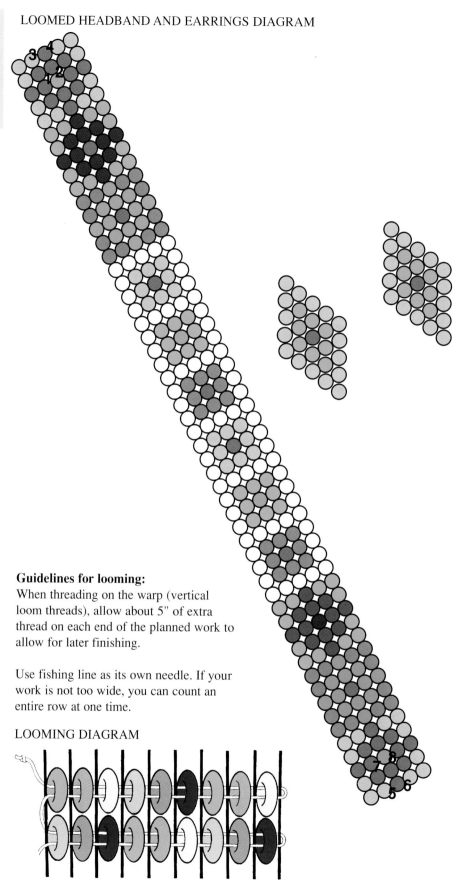

Materials
Beading loom
Nylon fishing line 25 lb. test
Plastic beads 4 mm: assorted pastel
    colors (325)
Earring hoop findings: gold (2)
Elastic cording: gold (30")
Plastic heart beads 10 mm: pink (2)

Directions
1. Using Loomed Headband and
Earrings Diagram as a pattern guide,
follow manufacturer's directions for
using loom.

2. For finishing headband, cut elastic
cording in two 15" pieces. Insert an end
of one piece of cording, from top side
of beaded design, between second and
third horizontal rows and between
second and third vertical rows at 1.
Insert an end of remaining piece of
cording, from top, between second and
third horizontal rows and between third
and fourth vertical rows at 2. Tie ends
of elastic cording together on underside
of design.

3. String free ends of cording as one
through one heart bead. Separate
cording pieces, and tie each around line
through first horizontal row of beads at
3 and 4.

4. Allowing enough cording to run the
length of beaded design, tie each free
end around line through last horizontal
row of beads at 5 and 6. On top side of
design, combine cording pieces as one,
and string through remaining heart
bead. Separate pieces and insert each at
7 and 8, respectively. Tie ends together
on underside of design.

5. For finishing earrings, insert hoop
finding through top bead. Repeat for
remaining earring.

Guidelines for looming:
When threading on the warp (vertical
loom threads), allow about 5" of extra
thread on each end of the planned work to
allow for later finishing.

Use fishing line as its own needle. If your
work is not too wide, you can count an
entire row at one time.

LOOMING DIAGRAM

*J*UDY LEHMAN, who is from Houston, Texas, holds a B.S. in art education. As an enthusiastic color and design specialist, Judy teaches Elementary Art, encouraging individual creativity and expression with all of her students. The children's artwork is often a source of inspiration to others, both children and adults. Judy is integrating basic art principles with computer technology in the classroom as an extension of the children's original work.

In the needlework world, Judy teaches, lectures, and judges for guilds and private workshops throughout the country. Certified in canvas and as a judge from the National Academy of Needlearts, she currently serves as the assistant director of the National Academy of Needleart's Teacher Certification Program and holds American Needlepoint Guild Fellow Level Credentials. She is a member of several professional organizations and distributes her commercial designs through Brite Ideas.

RAINBOW RING-AROUND

Stitched on Mono canvas 12, the finished design size is 5" x 6⅜". The fabric was cut 9" x 11". See Index for stitches.

Fabric	Design Size
Aida 11	5½" x 7½"
Aida 14	4¼" x 5⅞"
Aida 18	3⅜" x 4½"
Hardanger 22	2¾" x 3¾"

Materials
Mono canvas #12: 9" x 11" mounted on roller bars
Anchor pearl cotton #3: 133 blue (1 skein), 316 orange (1 skein), 46 red (1 skein), 110 violet (1 skein), 297 yellow (1 skein)
Persian wool, 3-ply: green (12 strands)
Tapestry needle #20 or #22
Scissors

Notes
Persian wool usually comes in good stitching lengths of about 22". One full strand has three smaller threads twisted together. Separate the three strands, and use two of them together in the needle.

Check overall diagram for center points of the 5" x 7" design area. The project is based on small square stitches which line up vertically and horizontally. Keeping the stitches lined up with one another is very important.

Various color combinations can be used with good end results for this project.

Anchor   DMC Pearl Cotton #3

Step 1: Smyrna Cross-Stitch (1 strand)
305   743 Yellow–med.

Step 2: Mosaic Stitch (1 strand)
110   208 Lavender–dk.

Step 3: Continental Stitch (1 strand)
316   740 Tangerine

Step 4: Cross-Stitch (2-ply)
N/A   Persian wool yarn, Green

Step 5: Mosaic Stitch (1 strand)
305   743 Yellow–med.

Step 6: Smyrna Cross-Stitch (1 strand)
46   666 Christmas Red

Step 7: Continental Stitch (1 strand)
133   796 Royal Blue–dk.
110   208 Lavender–dk.

RAINBOW RING-AROUND   Stitch Count: 60 x 82   Each grid square = 1 thread

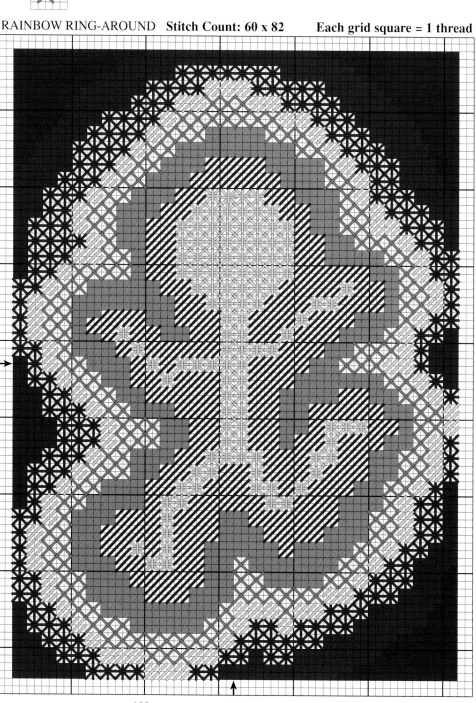

$\mathcal{R}$ibbon $\mathcal{E}$mbroidery

SPRING GARDEN

$\mathcal{S}$ HAY PENDRAY was nominated "Artist of the Year" and also "Entrepreneur of the Year" in her home state of Michigan.

Materials
Fabric: tea-dyed linen 20 ct.
Dressmaker's carbon
Embroidery hoop
Crewel needle #18
Silk ribbon and floss as outlined in
    Stitch Guide on opposite page

Directions
1. Transfer stitch design from Spring Garden Transfer Diagram, using dressmaker's carbon and following manufacturer's instructions.

2. Stretch fabric taut on a hoop before stitching.

3. Be sure to cover transfer lines on fabric completely when stitching. Do not clean until all stitching is completed, as transfer will be removed.

4. When using floss, separate six strands and refer to Stitch Guide on opposite page for number of strands to be used for each stitch.

5. Refer to Stitch Guide for stitch and color to be used (see Index for Stitches).

6. To end stitches, secure stitches in place for each flower or small area before beginning a new area. Tie a slip knot on wrong side of needlework to secure stitch in place and end ribbon.

SPRING GARDEN TRANSFER DIAGRAM

SPRING GARDEN STITCH DIAGRAM

Stitch Guide

Symbol	Stitch	Color	Size	Type
	Straight Stitch	Orange	4 mm	Silk
	Straight Stitch	267	6 strands	Anchor floss
	Couching Stitch	267	6 strands	Anchor floss
	Japanese Ribbon Stitch	Green	4 mm	Silk
	French Knot	Red	7 mm	Silk
	Straight Stitch	Red	7 mm	Silk
	French Knot	293	3 strands	Anchor floss
	Lazy Daisy Stitch	110	3 strands	Anchor floss
	Fly Stitch	108	2 strands	Anchor floss
	Outline Stitch	226	2 strands	Anchor floss
	Detached Wheatear Stitch with	50 52	6 strands 6 strands	Anchor floss Anchor floss
	Outline Stitch	267	3 strands	Anchor floss
	Straight Stitch wrapped with	358 358	6 strands 2 strands	Anchor floss Anchor floss
	Straight Stitch	118	6 strands	Anchor floss
	Japanese Ribbon Stitch	Lt. Blue	4 mm	Silk
	Buttons			
See Below	Mock Nun Stitch with top row	0875 129	#8 #8	Anchor pearl cotton Anchor pearl cotton

MOCK NUN STITCH

Worked to finish edges, the first journey begins by coming up at 1, going down at 2, coming up at 3, down at 4, and back up at 5. Continue in this manner until the edging is finished.

Returning to the point of 1 and 4, work a parallel stitch just below the first stitch. Come up at A, go down at B, up at C, continuing to the end of the edging.

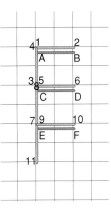

MARY JO HINEY has kept busy by authoring several how-to books and producing widely sought-after fabric-covered boxes.

Her background of eight years in the garment industry has afforded her with the ability to create a variety of different effects using a multitude of textures. As the owner of Something Special, Made by Hand, she manufactured gifts and decorative accessories for 11 years before writing *Victorian Ribbon and Lacecraft Designs* for Sterling Publishing in 1993. Since that time, she has worked on *Ribbon Basics* and wrote *Making Decorative Fabric Covered Boxes* for Sterling.

Currently, she is the owner of Bella Bella, a company that creates one-of-a-kind fineries.

WOVEN HEART

Materials

Velvet: black
   (7½" x 10½")
White paper: 8½" x 11"
   sheet (1)
Dressmaker's pen
Embroidery hoop
Crewel needle #18
Silk ribbon and floss, as
   outlined in Stitch
   Guide
Sewing thread: black
Bran buds: 1 cup

Directions

1. Using enlarged Woven Heart Stitch Diagram as pattern, cut two pin-keeper diamond shapes from velvet, adding ¼" all around for seams. Set one shape aside.

2. For black fabric, transfer stitch design from enlarged Woven Heart Transfer Diagram first on a white piece of paper and then trace with a dressmaker's pen, following manufacturer's instructions.

3. Stretch fabric taut on a hoop before stitching. Be sure to cover transfer lines on fabric completely when stitching. Do not clean until all stitching is completed, because transfer will be removed.

4. When using floss, separate six strands, and refer to Stitch Guide for number of strands to be used for each stitch.

5. Refer to Stitch Guide for stitch and color to be used (see Index for Stitches).

6. To end, secure stitches in place for each flower or small area before beginning a new area. Tie a slip knot on wrong side of needlework to secure stitch in place and end ribbon.

7. With right sides of velvet pieces together, sew a ¼" seam around diamond shape, leaving a 3" opening for stuffing. Turn right side out. Stuff with bran buds. Slip-stitch opening closed.

8. Tie a silk 7 mm bright pastel variegated bow at top of pin-keeper, as shown on Woven Heart Stitch Diagram. Cascade tails around.

Stitch Guide

Symbol	Stitch	Color	Size	Type
	Woven Ribbon	Pastel variegated	4 mm	Silk or Synthetic
	Couching Stitch	937	3 strands	DMC floss
	Couching Stitch	937	1 strand	DMC floss
	Lazy Daisy Stitch	Bright Pastel variegated	4 mm	Silk or Synthetic
	Free-Form Flower	Bright Pastel variegated	4 mm	Silk or Synthetic
	One-Twist Japanese Stitch	Lt. Green	4 mm	Silk or Synth.
	Cascading Stitch	Bright variegated	7 mm	Silk or Synthetic

WOVEN HEART STITCH DIAGRAM   **Enlarge 150%**

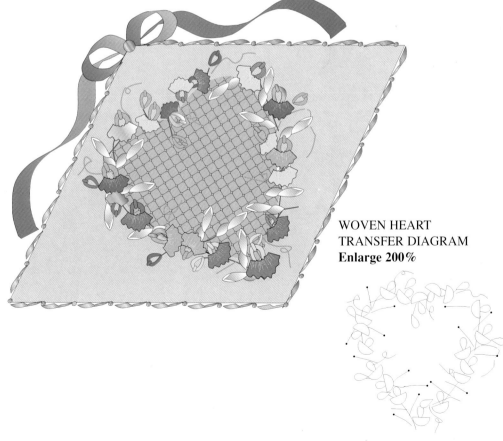

WOVEN HEART
TRANSFER DIAGRAM
Enlarge 200%

modern art form. She has been an embroiderer since childhood, only bringing this long experience to silk ribbon embroidery in 1984. Her artistic style combines a keen interest in gardening with an inherent creativity and unique ribbon handling techniques to produce floral works that rival those in nature.

Esther's works have been featured in *McCall's Needlework*, *Sew Beautiful*, and *Creative Needle*. Her book, *Esther's Silk Ribbon Embroidery*, is considered an essential primer. Most recently, she has completed an instructional video featuring a step-by-

step introduction into the world of silk ribbon embroidery as well as demonstrating the techniques described in her book. Additionally, Esther has taught silk ribbon embroidery classes and lectured at seminars throughout the United States as well as in England.

Esther's love of silk ribbon embroidery, her creativity, and her innovative techniques have added a new dimension to this time-honored art form and have ensured her recognition as a leader in its development.

*E*STHER RANDALL is known for her pioneering work in the revival of silk ribbon embroidery as a

ROSES CAMISOLE

Materials
Garment of choice
Dressmaker's carbon
Embroidery hoop
Crewel needle18"
Silk ribbon and floss,
    as outlined on
    Stitch Guide

Notes
It is necessary to stitch down the backs of the embroidery work so that the ribbon stitches will not come loose when the clothing is worn. Use a fine needle and thread to secure the stitches.

Directions
1. Transfer stitch design from enlarged Roses Camisole Transfer Diagram using dressmaker's carbon and following manufacturer's instructions.

2. Stretch fabric taut on a hoop before stitching.

3. Be sure to cover transfer lines on fabric completely when stitching. Do not clean until all stitching is completed because transfer will be removed.

4. When using floss, separate six strands and refer to Stitch Guide for number of strands to be used for each stitch.

5. Refer to Stitch Guide for stitch and color to be used (see Index for stitches).

Stitch Guide

Symbol	Stitch	Color	Size	Type
	Stem Stitch	Lt. Green	380	Denier Silk thread
	Feather Stitch	Lt. Green	380	Denier Silk thread
	Chain Stitch	Aqua	1000	Denier Silk thread
	Lazy Daisy Stitch	Green	4 mm	Silk
	Lazy Daisy Stitch	Aqua	4 mm	Silk
	French Knot	Yellow	4 mm	Silk
	Stem Stitch Rose	Pink	7 mm	Silk
	French Knot	Pink	7 mm	Silk
	Japanese Ribbon Stitch	Pink & Rose	7 mm	Silk
	French Knot	Pink & Rose	7 mm	Silk
	Japanese Ribbon Stitch	Rose	4 mm	Silk
	French Knot	Pink	4 mm	Silk

6. To end the stitches, secure stitches in place for each flower or small area before beginning a new area. Tie a slip knot on the wrong side of the needlework to secure the stitch in place and end ribbon.

ROSES CAMISOLE TRANSFER
DIAGRAM   **Enlarge 200%**

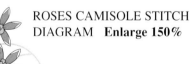

ROSES CAMISOLE STITCH
DIAGRAM   **Enlarge 150%**

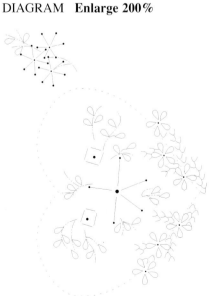

$\mathcal{K}$ATHERYN TIDWELL FOUTZ has always delighted in the creative process. She was raised in a very loving and supportive family who always encouraged her in her creative endeavors, which, more often than not, she says, ended up in disaster!

Katheryn enjoys designing, writing, and teaching many types of crafts, from doll-making to ribbon embroidery, across the United States, and is currently working on projects and designs for Singapore, London, and the Netherlands.

She has recently authored her first book, *Crafting with the New Ribbons,* a Sterling publication.

Katheryn believes that, in design, as in life, you should try to turn your stumbling blocks into stepping stones and never fret over making a mistake, but instead, find joy in the fact that you have created a new variation.

The creations which are most delightful to her are a collaborative work in progress with her husband, Kyle. Their children, who she decribes as "wonderful and amazing," are Rileigh Anne, Jason, and Katelyn.

IVORY BOUQUET VEST

Materials

Textured ribbon ⅜": gold (1 yd.)
Rayon ribbon ⅝": gold (1 yd.)
Sheer ribbon ⅝": gold (1 yd.)
Sheer ribbon ½": gold with gold edge
    (1 yd.)
Wired ribbon 1" wide: canvas with gold
    edge (1¼ yds.)
Mother-of-pearl buttons: small (8)
Woven vest: ivory
Transfer pen: air-soluble
Chenille needle #6 or #8
Beading needle
Sewing thread

Notes

When working with wide or textured ribbons, it is necessary to use a needle that is wide enough to thread ribbons through the eye as well as to have a body wide enough to create an opening for the ribbon to be pulled through. A tailor's awl can also be helpful.

After threading the appropriate needle, begin stitching by bringing the needle up from the back, leaving a ¾" tail. Tack down with a needle and thread. Upon completion of the design, bring ribbon to back side and tack end to secure. Trim any excess.

Directions

1. Using Ivory Bouquet Vest Stitch Diagram as pattern, trace design onto fabric with transfer pen. Make stems from very long Rolled Straight Stitches (see page 118 for "Rolled Straight Stitch") of textured ribbon. Hand-tack stems into place with tiny stitches with beading needle and thread.

2. Make rose leaves from rayon ribbon using the Bullion Lazy Daisy Stitch (see page 118).

3. To make each bud, cut a 4" length of wired and a 4" length of rayon ribbon (see page 118 for "Wrapped Bud"). Find center point of wired ribbon, and fold each end down and across ribbon in a downward direction. Run a hand-gathering stitch across the bottom and tighten gathers. Wrap bud in same manner with length of rayon ribbon and stitch. Wrap base of this bud tightly with a length of thread, and stitch to secure. Repeat for other bud.

4. Make rose by cutting a 30" length of wired ribbon. Tie a knot 1" from one end, forming a 1" stem. Carefully push ribbon back to expose wire at lower edge of ribbon. Grab onto wire and continue to push ribbon along wire toward knot, gathering ribbon tightly. Wind gathered edge of ribbon around and around stem just below knot. Fold cut edge of ribbon down and out of view so that no raw edges show. Wind the extending wire tightly around stem below gathers. Trim wire. Hand-stitch rose in place on design.

5. Lay each bud in place on design, and hand-stitch base onto the fabric. Using ⅜" textured ribbon, cover the raw edges of base with Straight Stitches (see page 37) placed side by side.

6. Hand-stitch buttons in place to accent the design as shown in Ivory Bouquet Vest Stitch Diagram.

7. Tie a bow in sheer gold ribbon with gold edge and knot tails at uneven intervals. Tack bow on bouquet stems.

IVORY BOUQUET VEST STITCH DIAGRAM   **Enlarge 135%**

BULLION LAZY DAISY STITCH

Bring the needle up at 1. Keep the ribbon flat, untwisted, and full. Put the needle down through fabric at 2 and up at 3, but do not pull through.

Loosely wrap ribbon around needle tip one to three times as indicated in stitch guide. Holding finger over wrapped ribbon, pull needle through ribbon.

CASCADING STITCH

The Cascading Stitch can be done starting with a bow or just using ribbon to "cascade" streamers through design. If starting with a bow, tie bow, leaving streamers long enough to work cascade through design. Thread streamer on needle, stitch down through fabric where bow placement is desired, and come back up at start of cascade effect. This will hold the bow in place. Come up at 1 and go down at 2. Come back up at 3, allowing ribbon to twist and lie loosely on the fabric. Go down again at 2 and come up at 3, making a small backstitch. This keeps the cascading in place.

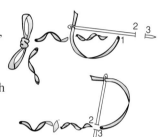

DETACHED WHEATEAR STITCH

This stitch consists of two Straight Stitches (see page 37) worked at right angles and a Lazy Daisy Stitch (see page 57) stitched over the base of these stitches. Keep all stitches straight and uniform.

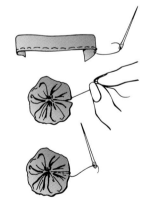

FREE-FORM FLOWER

Use a 2" piece of ribbon. Fold each end under about ⅛". Baste along one long edge of the ribbon with one strand of sewing thread or floss. Gently gather ribbon to create a petal the desired length. Knot to secure ruffled effect. Stitch ribbon in place along the gathered edge.

ONE-TWIST JAPANESE RIBBON STITCH

Follow instructions for Japanese Ribbon Stitch (see page 71), adding a twist in the ribbon before pushing the needle back down.

ROLLED STRAIGHT STITCH

Come up at 1; twist ribbon so that it rolls. Go down at 2, covering the desired length. Tack in place as desired.

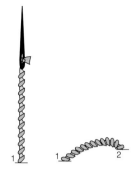

WOVEN RIBBON

Bring ribbon up through fabric, and make vertical Satin Stitches to fill shape. Begin horizontal Satin Stitches at top left of shape. Come up through fabric and weave ribbon over and under each vertical stitch. Upon reaching end of row, drop down one ribbon width and weave back across vertical stitches, alternating weave. Continue until shape is filled.

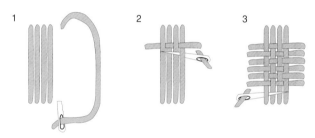

WRAPPED BUD

Cut a 4" length of ribbon. Lay a previously made bud in the center of the ribbon length. Cross one end of the 4" length of ribbon down and across the other end of the ribbon, wrapping the bud in the center. Run a gathering stitch across this wrapped piece. Pull the gathering thread tightly, and wrap the thread around the base. Knot to secure.

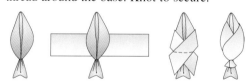

WRAPPED STRAIGHT STITCH

This stitch consists of a long vertical Straight Stitch which is crossed by short diagonal Straight Stitches. Come up at 1, and carry the thread up to 2. Insert the needle into fabric, and take a small stitch to the left at 3. Insert needle at 4, and stitch back up at 5. Continue along the line at even intervals to the end of the laid thread.

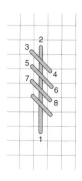

Overdyes

$\mathcal{F}$ROM THE INCEPTION of "The Embroidery Studio" television series, Pat Rozendal has worn many hats: design and technical coordinator, associate producer, author and/or editor of its books and leaflets. She has designed all of the previous series samplers and created the "Footnotes" segment, which she authors and presents.

An embroidery teacher for 20 years, she has taught for national embroidery seminars and individual groups across the nation. As an Embroiderers' Guild of America Master Craftsman in Canvas Work and a certified Master Judge, she has also judged local and national needlework exhibits across the country. Her designs have won numerous awards both locally and nationally, and "The Embroidery Studio" Series Samplers are all blue ribbon winners.

A graduate of the University of Houston with dual majors in Speech and Secondary Education, she and her husband, who is retired, live in Houston, Texas.

OLD-WORLD RUNNER

Stitched on white linen 26 over 2 threads, the finished design size is 14" x 38". The fabric was cut 43" x 19".

Stitch according to Old-World Runner Placement Diagram on opposite page and corresponding graphed sections on page 122. Diagram shows only one-half of completed design. Turn diagram upside down and continue stitching Sections 5, 6, 4, 3, 2, and 1. Do not repeat Section 7. See Index for stitches.

Section 1
Step 1: Cross-Stitch (2 strands)

 Overdyed floss, Mauve shades

Step 2: Backstitch (1 strand)

 Overdyed pearl cotton #8, Red shades

Step 3: Long Stitch (1 strand)

 Overdyed pearl cotton #8, Red shades

Section 2
Step 1: Eyelet Stitch (1 strand)

 Overdyed pearl cotton #8, Green/Brown shades

Step 2: Satin Stitch (3 strands)

 Overdyed floss, Yellow/Green shades

Step 3: Backstitch (1 strand)

 Overdyed pearl cotton #8, Green/Brown shades

Section 3
Step 1: Darning Stitch (3 strands)

 Overdyed floss, Lavender/Blue shades
Arrows indicate direction of stitch

Step 2: Parisian Stitch (1 strand)

 Overdyed pearl cotton #8, Mauve/Green shades

Step 3: Backstitch (1 strand)

 Overdyed pearl cotton #8, Mauve/Green shades

Section 4
Step 1: Cross-Stitch

 Overdyed floss, Mauve shades
/(2 strands), ½ cross, bottom stitch
\Overdyed pearl cotton #8, Mauve/Green shades, (1 strand), return stitch

Step 2: Backstitch (1 strand)

 Overdyed pearl cotton #8, Red shades

Section 5
Step 1: Darning Stitch, Horizontal (3 strands)

 Overdyed floss, Cream/Terra Cotta shades

Step 2: Florentine Stitch (3 strands)

 Overdyed floss, Terra Cotta/Dk.Terra Cotta shades
Cut darkest colors from skien

Step 3: Scotch Stitch, Vertical (3 strands)

 Overdyed floss, Green/Tan/Lt.Gray shades

Step 4: Milanese Stitch (3 strands)

 Overdyed floss, Violet shades

Step 5: Cross-Stitch (2 strands)

 Overdyed floss, Yellow/Green shades

Step 6: Backstitch (1 strand)

 Overdyed pearl cotton #8, Violet shades

Section 6
Step 1: Satin Stitch (3 strands)

 Overdyed floss, Cream/Terra Cotta shades

Step 2: Scotch Stitch, Horizontal (3 strands)

 Overdyed floss, Green/Tan/Lt.Gray shades

Step 3: Florentine Stitch (3 strands)

 Overdyed floss, Terra Cotta/Dk.Terra Cotta shades
Cut darkest colors from skien

Step 4: Scotch Stitch, Vertical (3 strands)

 Overdyed floss, Green/Tan/Lt.Gray shades

Step 5: Eyelet Stitch (1 strand)

 Overdyed pearl cotton #8, Lavender shades

Step 6: Cross-Stitch (2 strands)

 Overdyed floss, Yellow/Green shades

Step 7: Backstitch (1 strand)

 Overdyed pearl cotton #8, Lavender shades

Section 7
Step 1: Cross-Stitch (2 strands)

 Overdyed floss, Mauve shades

Step 2: Backstitch (1 strand)

 Overdyed pearl cotton #8, Red shades

Step 3: Long Stitch (1 strand)

 Overdyed pearl cotton #8, Red shades

OLD-WORLD RUNNER PLACEMENT DIAGRAM

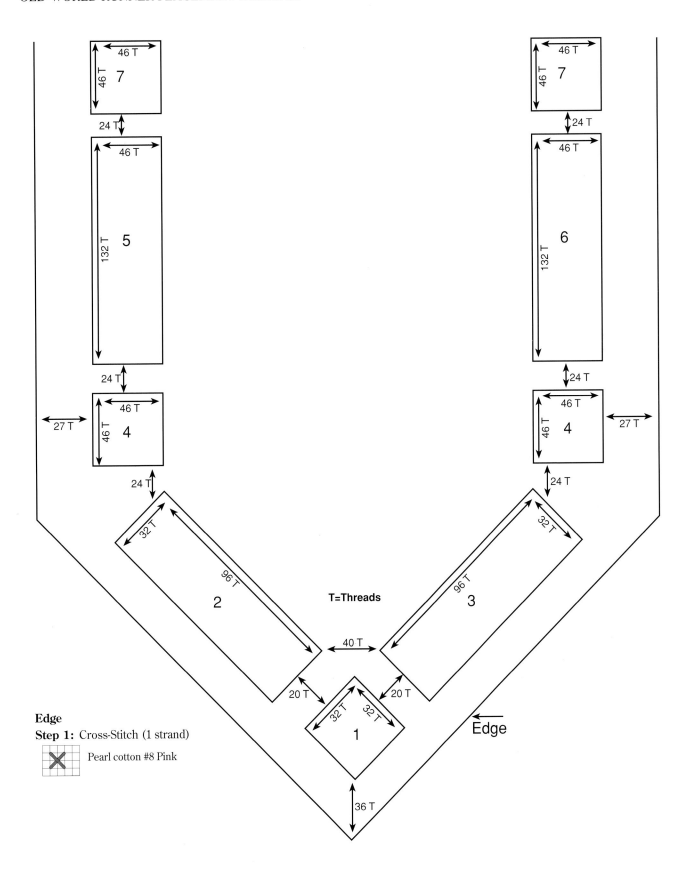

Edge

Step 1: Cross-Stitch (1 strand)

Pearl cotton #8 Pink

OLD-WORLD RUNNER GRAPH

Each grid square = 1 thread

Edge

*R*OSEMARY DRYSDALE was introduced at an early age to the world of pins, needles, and threads and the fine art of how to use them. She comes from a family of needleworkers and knitters. Her grandfather and mother were both professional dressmakers and her great-grandmother and grandmother were Scottish knitters. She studied needlework and embroidery in high school and attended the College of Home Economics at the University of Durham in Great Britain, graduating with the distinction of embroidery teacher.

Although Rosemary is an exceptional designer and has authored several books, booklets, and leaflets, teaching is her first love. Since the 1960s, she has been teaching, lecturing, and holding demonstrations at industry businesses and needlework shops throughout the country. Her aim is to instill in her students a love of embroidery and for them to think of it as a part of their everyday life and not as a separate art form.

Rosemary's immediate goal is to open a school near her eastern Long Island home in the country, where students can study needlework, take long walks, taste "good English food," and work in a relaxed atmosphere using the surrounding gardens for inspiration.

SPIRITED ORNAMENTS

Stitched on sand Cashel linen 28 over 2 threads, the finished design size is 2⅜" x 2⅜" for Ornament #1 and 2⅞" x 2⅞" for Ornament #2. The fabric for each was cut 6" x 6". See Index for stitches.

Ornament #1

Fabric	Design Size
Aida 11	3⅛" x 3⅛"
Aida 18	1⅞" x 1⅞"
Hardanger 22	1½" x 1½"

Ornament #2

Fabric	Design Size
Aida 11	3⅝" x 3⅝"
Aida 18	2¼" x 2¼"
Hardanger 22	1⅞" x 1⅞"

Overdyed Pearl Cotton #5

Step 1: Backstitch (1 strand)

 Blue/Orange/Red shades

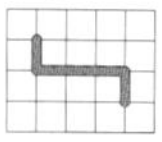

Step 2: Four-Sided Stitch (1 strand)

 Blue/Orange/Red shades

Step 3: Straight Stitch (1 strand)

Blue/Orange/Red shades

ORNAMENT #1   Stitch Count: 34 x 34
Each grid square = 2 threads

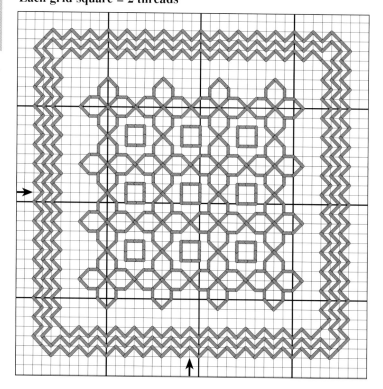

ORNAMENT #2   Stitch Count: 40 x 40
Each grid square = 2 threads

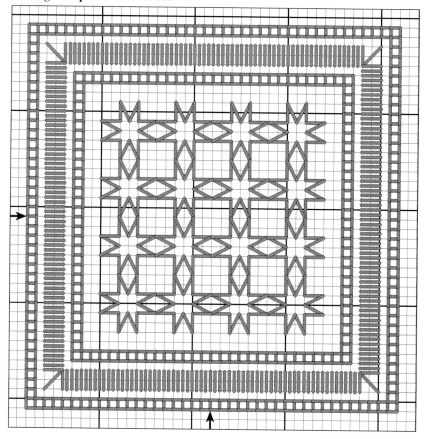

ANN CASWELL has been teaching needlework since 1979. She was shop manager for the American Needlework Guild from 1986 to 1991 and president-elect and president from 1993 to 1996.

A specialist, Ann works with more than 150 different types of threads. She has taught for shops and guilds across the United States and in Canada. Her focus is on knowing the variety of threads available on the market today, recognizing their properties, and demonstrating how they work in combination with each other. Additionally, Ann is very active in developing needlework graphics on the computer.

TEXTURED TEXTILES

Stitched on White Birch Heatherfield 16, the finished design size is 2" x 7¼". The fabric was cut 11" x 12". See Index for stitches.

Fabric	Design Size
Aida 11	3" x 10½"
Aida 14	2⅜" x 8¼"
Aida 18	1⅞" x 6⅜"
Hardanger 22	1½" x 5¼"

Notes

Plied threads can be used as they come from the strand or by alternating ends so that the color flow is not matched among the plies. If the plies are used as they come from the strand, an even flow of color results. If the thread color change is subtle, the effect is soft as demonstrated in the inner framework of the project.

But if the thread color change is more dramatic, as demonstrated in the outside regular edges of the design, a more noticeable change of color is seen. When the plies are reversed against each other, as demonstrated in the outside peaked edges of the design, a more mottled color change occurs. No one method is right or wrong—merely different. The stitcher can choose the desired effect.

"Less is more" is a useful axiom to remember when using multicolored threads. Too many colors can be confusing and sometimes disturbing to the eye. Remember to build in areas of solid and/or soft color in the design.

Overdyed Floss

Step 1: Diamond Fill-in Stitch (2 strands)

Lavender

Step 2: Double Straight Cross-Stitch (2 strands)

Overdyed pearl cotton #5 (1 strand),
Blue/Green shades

Blue/Lavender/Green shades
Combine the plies having the
color flow the same.

Blue/Lavender/Green shades
Combine the plies having the
color flow in opposite directions.

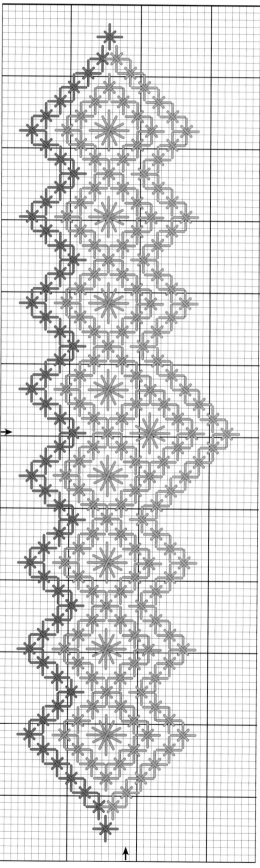

DOUBLE STRAIGHT CROSS-STITCH

This stitch consists of a larger upright cross topped with a smaller Cross-Stitch. Work in rows from left to right, then right to left, across area to be filled.

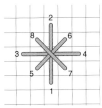

MILANESE STITCH

This stitch consists of rows of interlocking triangles. Stitch a Straight Stitch vertically over six threads of canvas. Then stitch over five threads, then four, then three, two and one. Begin again stitching pattern along lower diagonal of the triangle. Continue until filling a "star" shape.

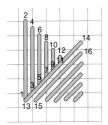

FLORENTINE STITCH

This stitch consists of uniform Straight Stitches worked in zigzag rows. Follow diagram sequence for first row; then work the next row with each stitch fitting next to the one above.

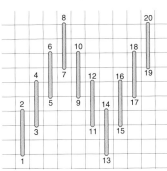

Metric Equivalency

MM-Millimetres   CM-Centimetres

INCHES TO MILLIMETRES AND CENTIMETRES

INCHES	MM	CM	INCHES	CM	INCHES	CM
⅛	3	0.3	9	22.9	30	76.2
¼	6	0.6	10	25.4	31	78.7
½	13	1.3	12	30.5	33	83.8
⅝	16	1.6	13	33.0	34	86.4
¾	19	1.9	14	35.6	35	88.9
⅞	22	2.2	15	38.1	36	91.4
1	25	2.5	16	40.6	37	94.0
1¼	32	3.2	17	43.2	38	96.5
1½	38	3.8	18	45.7	39	99.1
1¾	44	4.4	19	48.3	40	101.6
2	51	5.1	20	50.8	41	104.1
2½	64	6.4	21	53.3	42	106.7
3	76	7.6	22	55.9	43	109.2
3½	89	8.9	23	58.4	44	111.8
4	102	10.2	24	61.0	45	114.3
4½	114	11.4	25	63.5	46	116.8
5	127	12.7	26	66.0	47	119.4
6	152	15.2	27	68.6	48	121.9
7	178	17.8	28	71.1	49	124.5
8	203	20.3	29	73.7	50	127.0

$\mathcal{I}$ndex